Directions 2

BOOK TWO

Directions 2

BOOK TWO

DAVID JONES & GEOFF ROWLANDS

In association with
The Geographical Association

Hodder & Stoughton

A MEMBER OF THE HODDER HEADLINE GROUP

Acknowledgements

The publishers would like to thank the following for giving permission to reproduce copyright photographs in this book:

Alan Kinght, Figures 5/10.6c and d; David Kidney, Figures 5/2.5, 5/2.6; Trip Photos, Figures 2/1.5, 2/1.6, 3/4.5, 4/9.1abc, 5/10.5.

All other photos belong to the authors.

The authors would like to thank the following for their help and co-operation.

The Calvert family, Hazel Brow Farm; Dr. Alan J Knight, B&Q plc.

Every effort has been made to contact the holders of copyright material but if any have been inadvertently overlooked, the publisher will be pleased to make the necessary alterations at the first opportunity.

Inside artwork drawn by Phil Ford, Bitmap Graphics and Joe McEwan.

British Library Cataloguing in Publication Data

Jones, David
   Directions
   Book 2
   1.Geography
   I.Title II.Rowlands, Geoff
   910

   ISBN 0 340 64766 3

First published 1996
Impression number   10 9 8 7 6 5 4 3 2 1
Year   1999 1998 1997 1996

Typeset by Wearset, Boldon, Tyne and Wear.
Printed in Malaysia for Hodder & Stoughton Educational, a division of Hodder Headline Plc, 338 Euston Road, London NW1 3BH
by Times Offset (M) sdn Bnd.

CONTENTS

PEOPLE AND THE NATURAL ENVIRONMENT

Water

main idea

Water is an essential resource

1 Make a list of problems or issues to do with water. The headlines in Figure 1 will give you a start.

2 a) Make a list of all the ways in which you use water in a day. Compare your list with those of other people in your class.

b) How much water do you think you use in a day?

Figure 1
Newspaper headlines

High Death Toll in Italy's Floods

Country Braced for Fresh Floods

New Plans For Giant Reservoirs

Heatwave Deepens Drought

Hosepipe and Sprinkler Bans

key words

relief rain
rain shadow
depressions
water surplus
water shortage
water supplies

Rainfall in Britain

In Britain rainfall is higher in the west and becomes lower the further east you go. This is because:

- mountains are in the west and produce **relief rain**;
- lowlands are to the east in the **rain shadow** (see Book 1, Chapter 1, Unit 5);
- rain-bearing weather systems called **depressions** come from the west.

3 Look at the two maps of Britain in Figures 3 and 4. Using a blank map of Britain:

a) shade in the areas which you think have more water than they need (**water surplus**);

b) shade in the areas which you think have little water (**water shortage**);

c) give three reasons why the water surplus areas have plenty of water;

d) give three reasons why the water shortage areas do not have enough water.

Figure 2
Clywedog Reservoir

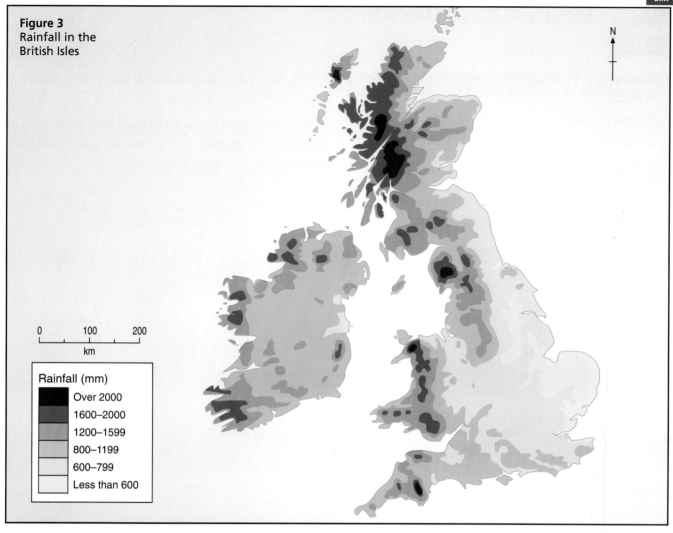

Figure 3
Rainfall in the British Isles

0   100   200
km

Rainfall (mm)
- Over 2000
- 1600–2000
- 1200–1599
- 800–1199
- 600–799
- Less than 600

N

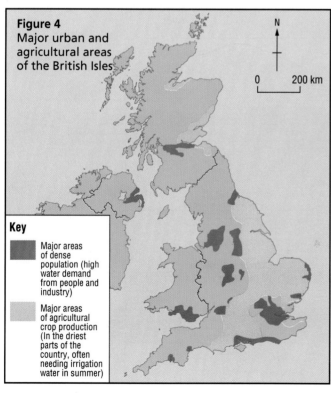

Figure 4
Major urban and agricultural areas of the British Isles

N

0   200 km

Key
- Major areas of dense population (high water demand from people and industry)
- Major areas of agricultural crop production (In the driest parts of the country, often needing irrigation water in summer)

Water supplies

Our **water supplies** come from several sources.
- Water may be taken from rivers, usually near the place where it is needed.
- Water may be taken from rocks underground, again usually where the water is needed.
- Water may be piped from reservoirs, which are mostly in the mountain areas.
- Water may be stored in reservoirs, then released into rivers, and taken from the rivers near where the water is needed.

Rivers and floods

main idea

▼

Rivers move water to the sea.

Rivers take rain water back to the sea. Figure 1 shows how this happens.

The features of the **river basin** affect how quickly the rain water reaches the river and the route it takes to get there.

Figure 1
River basin
water movement
system

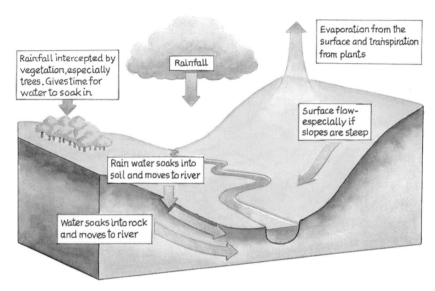

Figure 2
Water movement

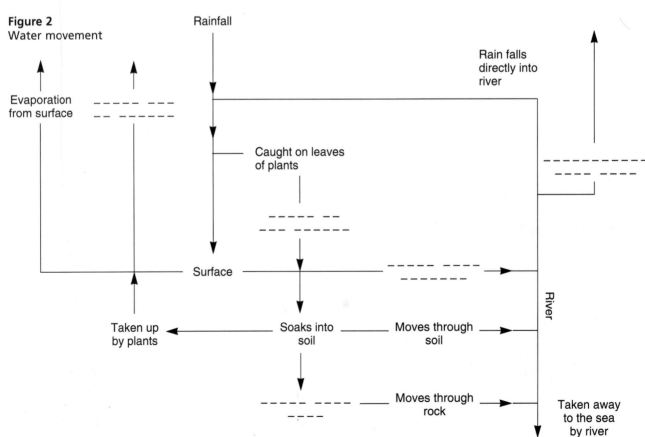

1 Look at the block diagram of the river basin in Figure 1. Make a large copy of the flow chart (Figure 2). Use the labels below to finish it.

Flows over surface; Soaks into rock; Evaporation from river; Drips to the ground; Given off by plants.

2 Use your finished version of Figure 2 to answer the following questions.
   a) How many different routes can rain water take to the river?
   b) Name the different routes.
   c) Which routes do not take water to the river?

The amount of water there is and how quickly it reaches the river are important points. If a lot of water gets to the river quickly then the river level will rise quickly. This could mean **flooding**.

The photographs in Figures 3 and 4 show the River Wye at Ross-on-Wye in Gwent. The map in Figure 5 shows the river basin of the Wye.

Figure 5
The Wye river basin

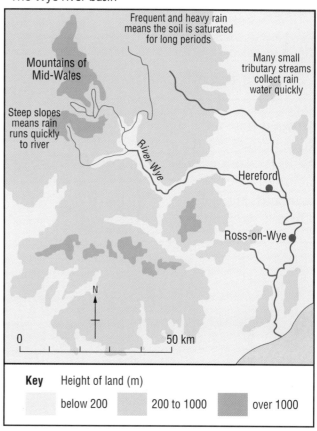

Frequent and heavy rain means the soil is saturated for long periods

Mountains of Mid-Wales

Many small tributary streams collect rain water quickly

Steep slopes means rain runs quickly to river

River Wye

Hereford

Ross-on-Wye

N

0   50 km

Key   Height of land (m)
        below 200   200 to 1000   over 1000

Figure 3
Low water in the River Wye at Ross-on-Wye

3 a) Study the labels on Figure 5 and copy and complete the following passage.

The River Wye rises in the _____ of Mid-Wales. As a result there are often times when the whole river basin has long periods of heavy _____. With steep _____ and often thin soils rain water reaches the river _____. Long periods of rain also mean that the soil is _____ so rain runs off to the river even more quickly. Snow melting is another cause of river levels rising quickly.

b) Explain why the flooding in Figures 3 and 4 happens almost every winter.

Figure 4
River Wye at Ross-on-Wye in flood

key words
river basin
flooding

The Mississippi flood

main idea

Flooding can affect large areas.

Between June and August 1993 the Mississippi River in the USA flooded. When it burst its banks it swamped a huge area of land. This included cities like Des Moines as well as farmland. Figure 1 shows the parts that were officially declared disaster areas.

1 Study Figure 1 of the Mississippi River basin and an atlas map of the USA.
   a) How many states are part of the Mississippi River basin?
   b) How many of the states were in the disaster area?
   c) Which states were worst affected?

Figure 1
Mississippi River flood

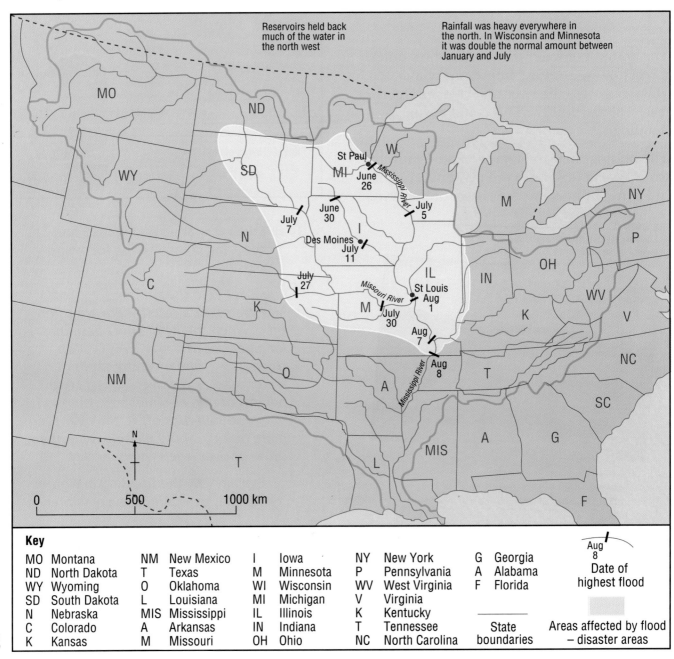

Key

MO	Montana	NM	New Mexico	I	Iowa	NY	New York	G	Georgia
ND	North Dakota	T	Texas	M	Minnesota	P	Pennsylvania	A	Alabama
WY	Wyoming	O	Oklahoma	WI	Wisconsin	WV	West Virginia	F	Florida
SD	South Dakota	L	Louisiana	MI	Michigan	V	Virginia		
N	Nebraska	MIS	Mississippi	IL	Illinois	K	Kentucky		
C	Colorado	A	Arkansas	IN	Indiana	T	Tennessee		
K	Kansas	M	Missouri	OH	Ohio	NC	North Carolina		

Aug
8
Date of
highest flood

Areas affected by flood
– disaster areas

State boundaries

2 a) Use an outline copy of Figure 1. Shade in the area that was flooded in June. Using another colour, shade in the area flooded in July, and in a third colour, the area flooded in August.

b) How did places downriver have an advantage when it came to flood warning?

c) Why were the north and west saved from the worst flooding?

d) Why was there so little flooding to the south of Illinois and Missouri?

e) What do you think was the reason for the rise in the level of the river?

3 Look at Figure 2.

a) List all of the changes shown.

b) For each change say what the advantage is. Think about times of high, average and low rainfall.

c) For each change say what the disadvantage is. Again, think about times of high, average and low rainfall.

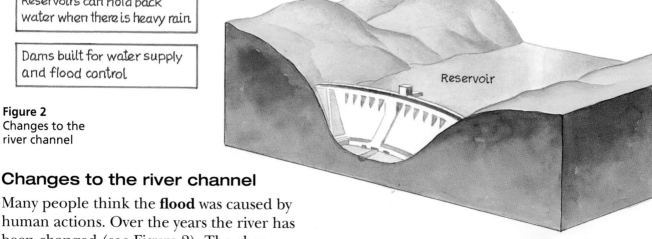

Old path of river

a

New path – river straightened; embankments or levées to hold water in channel

Water moves more quickly. If it meets high water coming down another tributary, flooding could happen

River channel may be dredged to keep it deep enough for river barges. This also speeds up water flow

b

Reservoirs can hold back water when there is heavy rain

Dams built for water supply and flood control

Reservoir

Figure 2
Changes to the river channel

Changes to the river channel

Many people think the **flood** was caused by human actions. Over the years the river has been changed (see Figure 2). The changes have speeded up water movement along the river.

Because of the changes water now builds up in the **river channel**. Once it reaches the top of the **levées** it overflows and floods the surrounding land.

key words

flood
river channel
levées

Rivers and landforms

Rivers change the shape of the land.

Rivers produce different **landforms** along their courses. They do this by:

- **erosion** (wearing away);
- **transportation** (moving);
- **deposition** (dropping).

1 Look at Figure 1.
  a) In what three ways does a river erode?
  b) Describe the shape of the upper valley.
  c) In which part of the valley is the **gradient** (slope) most gentle?
  d) What feature is formed when a meander is cut off?
  e) What feature is found where a band of resistant rock cuts across a valley?

Figure 1
Changes along a valley

	Upper valley	Middle valley	Lower valley
Valley slope (gradient)	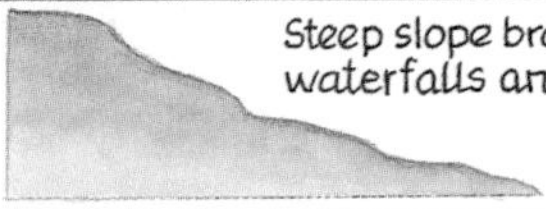 Steep slope broken by waterfalls and rapids	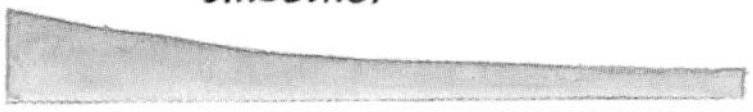 Gentle gradient, much smoother	 Very gentle and smooth gradient, almost flat
Valley shape (cross-section)	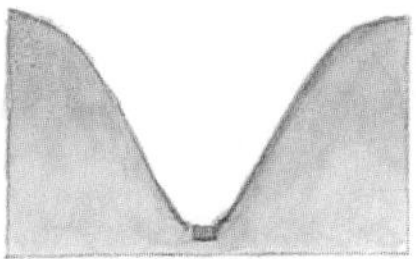 Steep-sided and narrow, sometimes vertical sides (gorge)	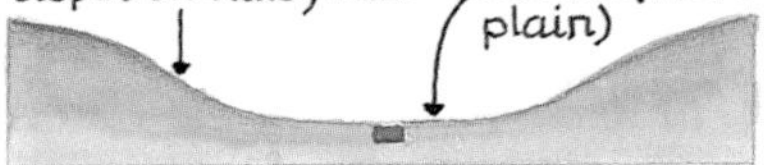 Lower, more gentle slopes on valley side / Flat valley bottom (flood plain)	 Wide flat valley bottom (flood plain)
Land forms — Large-scale, Medium-scale, Small-scale	Interlocking spurs formed as valley winds from side to side / Waterfalls, formed where harder bands of rock occur / Pot-holes where river cuts down into river bed	Wider, straighter valley with flat bottom (flood plain) River meanders / Erosion by undercutting on outside of bend / Deposition / a. Deep, fast moving / b. Shallower, slower flowing	Very wide flood plain 'cut-off' meanders (ox-bow lakes) / Alluvium covered / Mud flats at low tide / Sea / Estuary
Processes erosion transport deposition	Mostly vertical erosion - cutting down making deep steep-sided valley. Three kinds of erosion: Corrosion or abrasion - river bed worn away by boulders and pebbles. Attrition - boulders and pebbles wear down by knocking against each other and river bed. Hydraulic action - force of flood water tears out bits of rock	Erosion is sideways (lateral) as well as vertical. Deposition is when river load of pebbles, sand and silt is dropped when river level falls. At flood times the flat land on either side of river is flooded (the flood plain) and alluvium is deposited (sand, silt and clay)	Virtually no erosion. River transports mostly mud, silt and sand. Meanders make complicated patterns. Cut-offs or ox-bow lakes form when river changes course. This happens at time of flood. River estuary shows much deposition of sand and mud

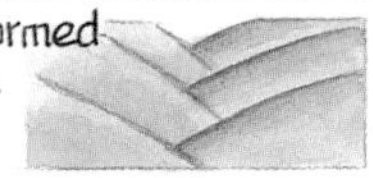

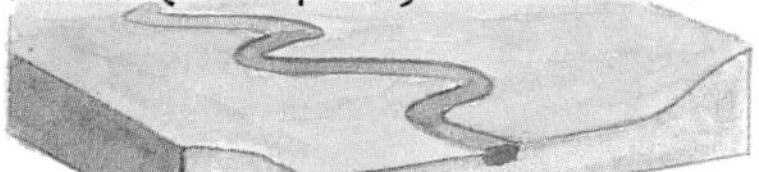

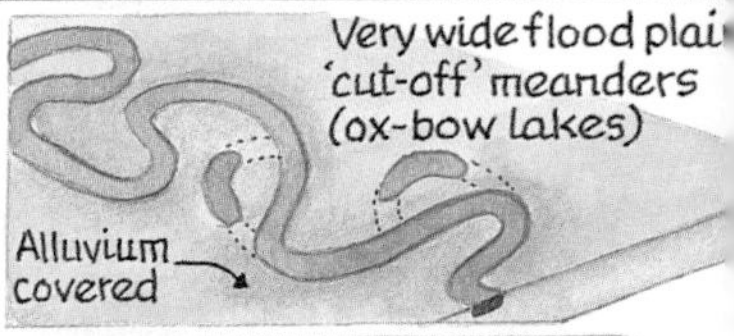

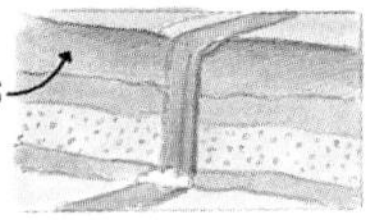

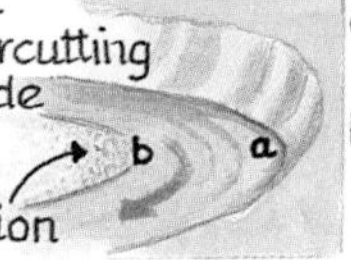

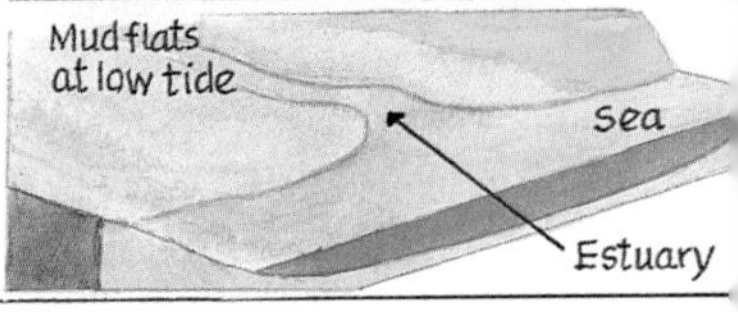

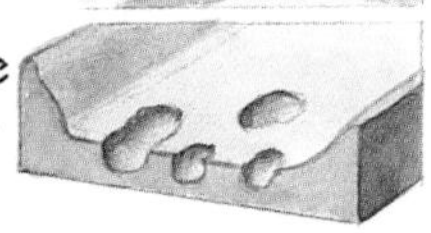

2 Study the photographs in Figure 2 and the map in Figure 3.

Take each one in turn. Say what feature is shown and how it has been formed.

3 Figure 3 shows the locations of the photographs in Figure 2. Match the photographs to the most likely locations.

Erosion takes place when river levels are high. This is also the time when eroded rock is transported down the valley. When river levels fall the material is deposited.

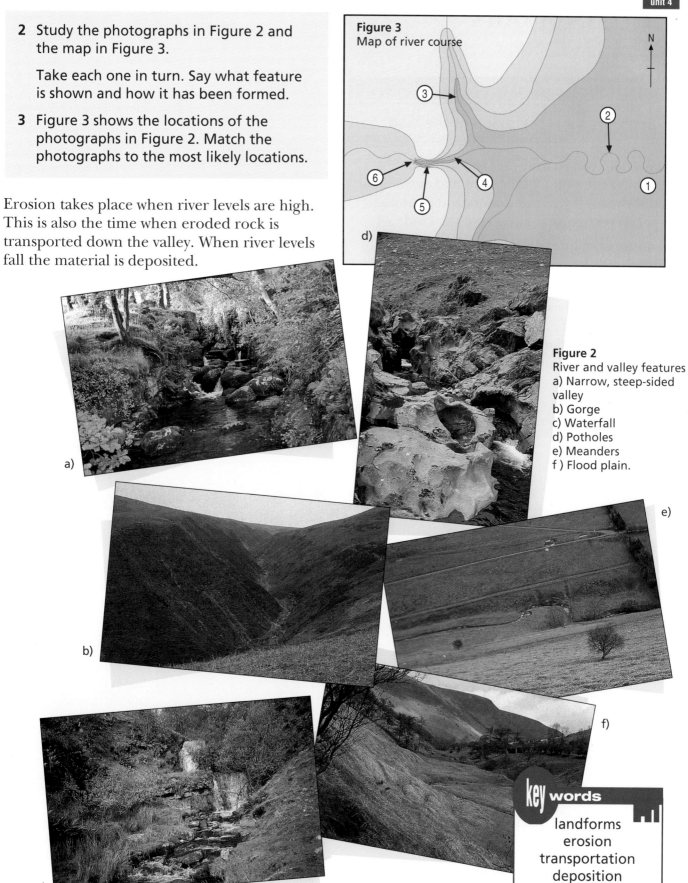

Figure 3
Map of river course

Figure 2
River and valley features
a) Narrow, steep-sided valley
b) Gorge
c) Waterfall
d) Potholes
e) Meanders
f) Flood plain.

key words
landforms
erosion
transportation
deposition
gradient

main idea

Contours show the shape of the land.

Maps help you to find your way around. Knowing the shape of the land makes using maps easier. If you can understand contours you can recognise the shape of the land.

Contours are lines on a map which join places of the same height. The height is usually given in metres above sea level (see Figure 1).

Steep and **gentle** slopes can be identified using contours. If there are no contours, it means that the land is **flat**. Lots of contours close together mean that the slope is steep.

Figure 1
A contour

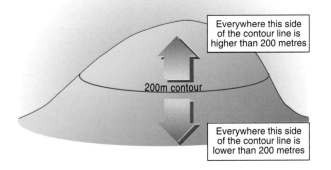

Everywhere this side of the contour line is higher than 200 metres

200m contour

Everywhere this side of the contour line is lower than 200 metres

1 Look at Figure 2. How are the contours different for steep and gentle slopes?

Figure 2
Steep and gentle slopes

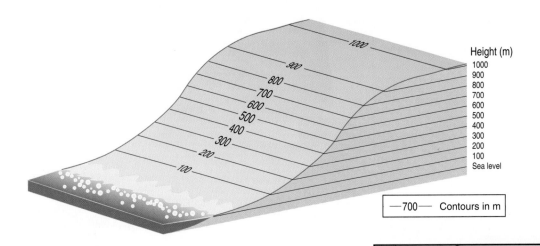

Height (m)
1000
900
800
700
600
500
400
300
200
100
Sea level

—700— Contours in m

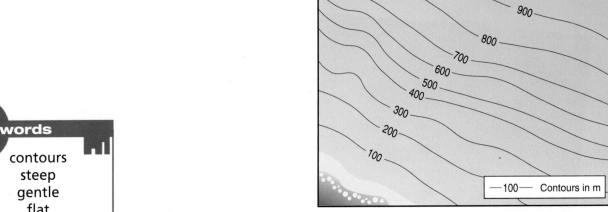

—100— Contours in m

key words
contours
steep
gentle
flat

14

Figure 3
Views of a
river course

a)

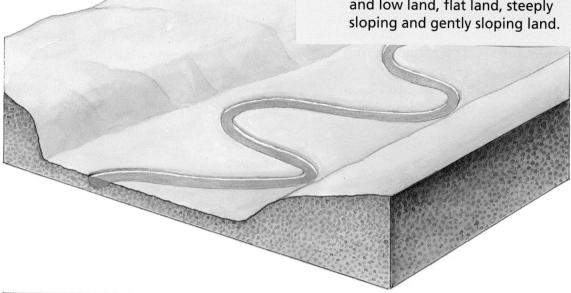

2 Use a copy of Figure 3b).
   a) Colour the *low* area of *flat* land in
       yellow.
   b) Colour the *high* area of *gently sloping*
       land in red.
   c) Colour the *steep* slope in green.
   d) Use the words in italics in parts a), b)
       and c) of this question to label your
       map. This shows you can identify high
       and low land, flat land, steeply
       sloping and gently sloping land.

b)

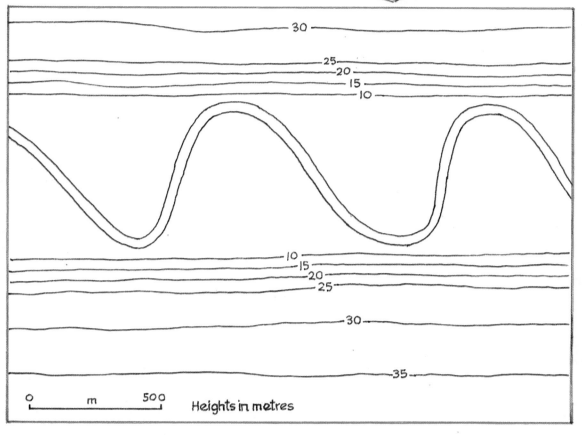

Heights in metres

Natural hazards

Natural hazards put many people at risk.

A **hazard** is some kind of event which puts people or places at **risk**. People face many different hazards or risks. Some are purely natural hazards; some are the result of human activity; and some are a combination of the two. One example of a natural hazard is an earthquake. The result of a hazard like an earthquake is often a **disaster**, with damage and death.

Figure 1
Human and natural hazards

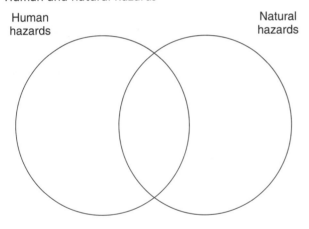

Human hazards   Natural hazards

1 a) Make a large copy of Figure 1. Write each hazard from Figure 2 in the appropriate place on your copy of Figure 1.
   b) Add some extra hazards of your own.
   c) Underneath the diagram write down the items you found difficult to place.

   Discuss the reasons for this. Would these go in the overlapping part of your diagram?

key words

hazard
risk
disaster

The map in Figure 3 shows areas of the world affected by three types of natural hazard: earthquakes; volcanoes; and tropical storms (hurricanes).

2 Look at Figure 3 and an atlas.
   a) Which areas of the world are affected by at least one of the hazards?
   b) Name some areas which are affected by all three hazards.
   c) Name ten major cities which are at risk from all three hazards.

Figure 2
Possible hazards

River floods	Hurricanes
Earthquakes	Volcanic eruptions
Landslides	Drought
Forest fires	Oil leaks
Fog	Ice
Sea floods	Soil erosion
Toxic waste	Sea wall collapse
Nuclear explosion	↑
War	Terrorism
Air, road, rail, sea disasters	↑
Chemical fires	
Heat	Storm surge

Large numbers of people live in areas where there is a risk of natural disaster. The reason they stay is simple. These areas have other attractions.

Some have fertile soils, which are formed from volcanic rocks and a warm, moist tropical climate. Agriculture can support large numbers of people in areas like this. The island of Java in Indonesia is an example.

Other areas have an attractive and pleasant climate which has attracted people, such as California in the USA.

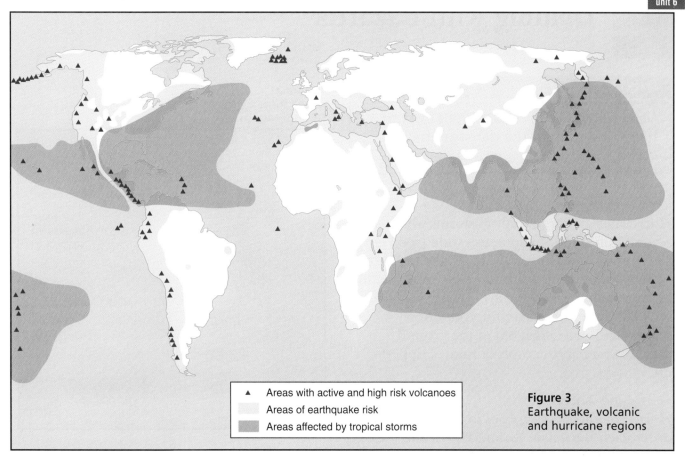

Figure 3
Earthquake, volcanic and hurricane regions

Legend:
▲ Areas with active and high risk volcanoes
Areas of earthquake risk
Areas affected by tropical storms

What are the risks?

Figure 4 shows some of the world's strongest earthquakes. The number of people killed varies enormously, but gives us some idea of the results in human terms.

There are other problems.

- Survivors in isolated areas may be cut off from help. This is made worse if roads, bridges and railways are destroyed.
- Then there is the difference between economically developed countries and economically developing countries. The former have the resources to deal with problems quickly. In economically developing countries these resources are often lacking. Survivors, even in accessible places, may not get help.
- Even in economically developed countries there is a period of chaos after a natural disaster. In the Kobe earthquake in Japan in 1995 gas pipes burst and caused raging fires. Burst water pipes meant that the fire service had no water to fight the fires.

4 Look at Figure 4.
   a) Compare the numbers of casualties in the earthquakes in economically developed and economically developing regions.
   b) Suggest reasons for the differences.

Figure 4
Some of the world's major earthquakes

Year	Place	Number of deaths
1995	Kobe, Japan	5200
1994	Los Angeles, California	60
1993	Latur, India	9750
1990	Western Iran	50 000
1988	Armenia	25 000
1985	Mexico City, Mexico	9500
1980	Algeria	4500
1976	Tangshan, China	655 000
1970	Northern Peru	67 000
1964	Southern Alaska	131

Dealing with hazards

Making plans can reduce the effect of hazards and limit the damage they cause.

Hurricanes

Hurricanes are large tropical storms which are several hundreds of kilometres wide (see Figure 1). Winds which often have speeds of well over 120 km an hour blow around the centre of the storm which is called the eye. Where hurricanes cross land they can cause huge amounts of damage – trees torn out of the ground, cars blown away, the roofs of houses ripped off.

Hurricane Andrew

Hurricanes are given names in alphabetical order each hurricane season. Hurricane Andrew hit the USA in August 1992. It caused more damage than any other hurricane in the previous 50 years. The repair bill was estimated at £15 billion. Whole towns were destroyed.

Before hitting the coast of the Gulf of Mexico it crossed a number of oil fields. 43 oil rigs were completely blown over, 125 were left leaning and nearly 400 pipelines were damaged.

Figure 2
A sea surge in the Gulf of Mexico

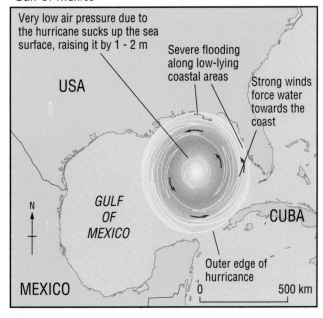

Very low air pressure due to the hurricane sucks up the sea surface, raising it by 1 - 2 m

Severe flooding along low-lying coastal areas

Strong winds force water towards the coast

USA

N

GULF OF MEXICO

CUBA

Outer edge of hurricane

MEXICO

0   500 km

Severe flooding was caused along the coast by **sea surges** (see Figure 2).

However, fewer than 40 people were killed. This was partly due to the **forecasting** and tracking of the storm. With advance warning people had time to get to safety. In a developed country there is enough money for warning systems.

Figure 1
Tropical storms: where they are and what they are called

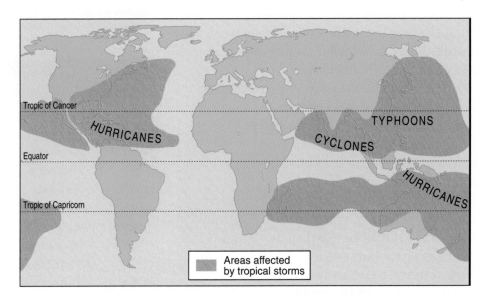

Tropic of Cancer

HURRICANES

TYPHOONS

CYCLONES

Equator

HURRICANES

Tropic of Capricorn

Areas affected by tropical storms

Figure 3
Map of Hurricane
Andrew's track

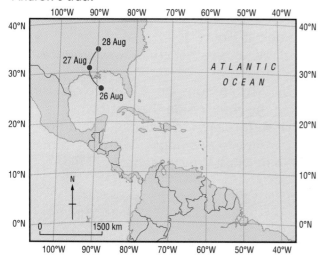

1 Use a large copy of Figure 3 and an atlas.
   a) On your map plot the track of the hurricane using the latitude and longitude information in Figure 4.
   b) Label these areas on your map: The Leeward Islands; South America; The Bahamas; The Gulf of Mexico; Louisiana.
   c) Which part of the USA was first hit by the hurricane? Add its name to your map.
   d) Label the coastal area flooded by sea surges.

Figure 4
Hurricane Andrew's track

Date (1992)	Latitude and longitude
18 August	14°N 46°W
19 August	16°N 53°W
20 August	20°N 60°W
21 August	24°N 63°W
22 August	26°N 66°W
23 August	26°N 71°W
24 August	26°N 77°W
25 August	27°N 84°W
26 August	On Figure 3
27 August	On Figure 3
28 August	On Figure 3
29 August	37°N 87°W

Thames Barrier

Many parts of the British coast are at or near sea level. Some, like the Fens in East Anglia, are below sea level. Most have to be protected from flooding.

London needed to be protected from steadily rising tides, so **embankments** were raised over the years. However, London could have been flooded if all the following had happened together:
- a sea or storm surge causing sea level to rise by 1 m or more;
- storm winds from the north pushing water towards the narrow end of the North Sea and the Thames estuary;
- high river water levels meeting a high tide coming upstream;
- spring tides (higher than usual tides).

The Thames Barrier was built to stop tidal water coming upstream. At times of flood danger the gates of the barrier can be closed. High embankments have been built to protect areas downstream.

Figure 5 The Thames barrier

2 Look at Worksheet 2/1.7 and the conditions for flooding listed above.
   a) Complete the labels to explain the flood danger.
   b) Why do the areas of downstream London also need flood defences?

Local hazards

Even small-scale, local hazards can cause major problems

Weather hazards are a special problem for travellers. **Fog**, snow, ice and strong winds are all problems at different times.

1 Look at Figure 1.
   a) What weather conditions produce fogs?
   b) Why are fogs more likely to occur in the countryside than in towns?
   c) Before laws to cut smoke pollution, thick fogs (**smogs**) used to be common in cities. Why was that?

Figure 1
Formation of fog

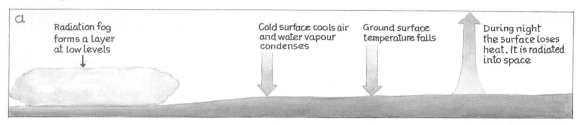

a Radiation fog forms a layer at low levels

Cold surface cools air and water vapour condenses

Ground surface temperature falls

During night the surface loses heat. It is radiated into space

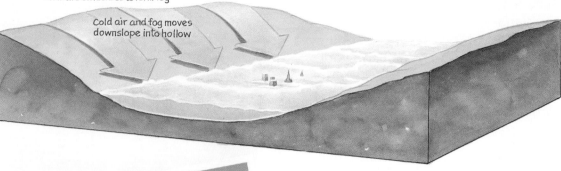

b Ground surface cooled as heat is radiated into space

Air cooled by cold ground surface. Moisture condenses to form fog

Fog builds up in hollow

Cold air and fog moves downslope into hollow

Figure 2
Fog hollow

Frost makes icy patches on pavements and roads and causes many accidents (see Figure 3).

Figure 3
Icy patches on roads

Cold clear night in winter - ground surface temperature falls. Road loses heat more quickly than surrounding woods and fields. Temperature of air in contact with road drops below freezing point. Condensation of water vapour directly forms ice

Icy road surface

No frost on fields

2 Look at Figure 3.
   a) Why is frost more likely if there is a clear sky at night?
   b) Explain why a clear winter night after rain makes icy conditions even more likely.

Sometimes in winter the weather stays the same for days on end. This is when there is an **anticyclone** or area of high pressure. Clear skies are then common.

One result of this is a **temperature inversion**. This means that it is colder at ground level than 100 m or so up into the air. The cold air is heavy and stays there. Fogs often form. **Pollution** in the air gets trapped by the inversion. It is a major problem for people with chest and breathing problems.

From high viewpoints you can see the pollution forming a brown layer near the top of the fog. The longer the fog lasts the thicker the polluted layer becomes.

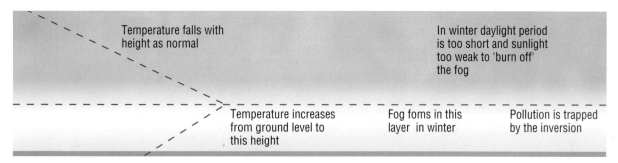

Figure 4 Temperature inversion, fog and trapped pollution

Figure 5 Inversion fog over Stafford

3 Look at Figures 4 and 5. Use a copy of Figure 6.
   a) Add these labels to your picture.
   - *Fog formed where cold air collects in valleys.*
   - *Layer of fog over city.*
   - *Pollution layer in fog.*
   b) Why are the people at the top of the block of flats in sunshine and the ones at the bottom in fog?

Figure 6
Different experiences of weather

key words

fogs
smog
frost
anticyclone
temperature inversion
pollution

21

Earthquakes and volcanoes

Earthquakes and volcanoes occur at plate edges

The **earth's crust** is not one solid layer. It is broken into sections called **plates**. These plates move. Volcanic and earthquake activity occurs at their boundaries.

The Japanese earthquake on 17 January 1995 at the city of Kobe measured 7.2 on the Richter scale (see Figure 2). It caused enormous damage and killed over 5000 people. There was damage up to 100 km away.

Japan is on a part of the earth's crust which is very active and so earthquakes are common there.

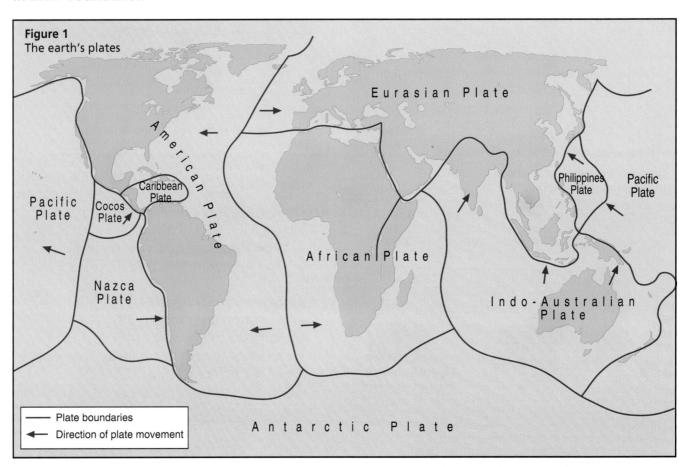

Figure 1
The earth's plates

Eurasian Plate

American Plate

Caribbean Plate

Pacific Plate

Cocos Plate

Philippines Plate

Pacific Plate

Nazca Plate

African Plate

Indo-Australian Plate

Antarctic Plate

— Plate boundaries
← Direction of plate movement

You will notice that **volcanoes** and **earthquakes** are found in the same areas as the boundaries of the plates.

Sudden movements of shifting plates cause **shock waves**. These are earthquakes. The effects are greatest immediately above where the shock started. The ground moves and buildings may collapse. The most powerful earthquakes may even damage buildings that have been specially built to withstand earthquakes.

1 Trace the plate boundaries from Figure 1. Put your tracing over Figure 3 in Unit 6. How do the patterns compare?

The Philippines Plate and the Pacific Plate are moving towards Japan. They are forced down beneath the Eurasian Plate (see Figure 3).

A sudden movement of these plates caused the Kobe earthquake (Figure 4).

Figure 2
Measuring earthquakes

Earthquake strength is measured in several ways. The media usually use the Richter scale.	
Richter	**Effects**
2	Smallest felt earthquake (feel it sitting or lying down).
4.5 to 5	Local damage (crockery rattles, ground shakes, some damage).
7 and over	Major earthquake (damage to buildings and roads, ground cracks).
7.75 and over	Greatest earthquakes (total devastation).

Earthquakes can also happen where the plates move away from each other and where they slide past each other (Figure 5).

Volcanoes occur at plate boundaries because molten material called magma is able to force its way to the surface here.

> **2** On what sort of plate boundary are the volcanoes of:
> a) the Andes of South America;
> b) Japan;
> c) Indonesia;
> d) Iceland;
> e) the Azores?
> Look at Figures 3 and 5 to help you.

Figure 3
The destructive or converging plate boundary in the Kobe area

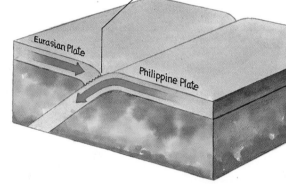

Friction zone – earthquakes happen here when pressure builds up and the plates shift suddenly

Eurasian Plate

Philippine Plate

Figure 5
a) Constructive or diverging plate boundaries in the Atlantic Ocean
b) Transform fault on the west coast of the USA

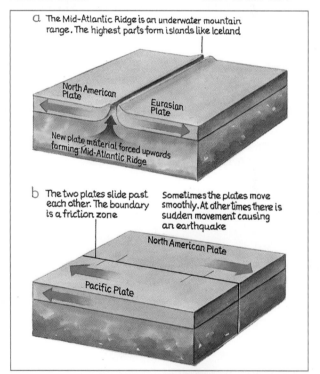

a The Mid-Atlantic Ridge is an underwater mountain range. The highest parts form islands like Iceland

North American Plate

Eurasian Plate

New plate material forced upwards forming Mid-Atlantic Ridge

b The two plates slide past each other. The boundary is a friction zone

Sometimes the plates move smoothly. At other times there is sudden movement causing an earthquake

North American Plate

Pacific Plate

Figure 4
Kobe and the effect of the earthquake

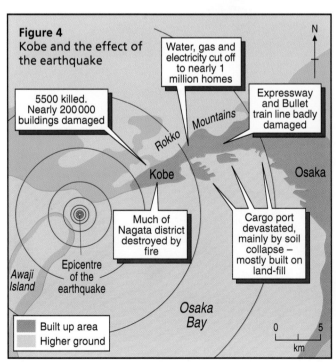

N

Water, gas and electricity cut off to nearly 1 million homes

Expressway and Bullet train line badly damaged

5500 killed. Nearly 200 000 buildings damaged

Rokko Mountains

Kobe

Osaka

Much of Nagata district destroyed by fire

Cargo port devastated, mainly by soil collapse – mostly built on land-fill

Awaji Island

Epicentre of the earthquake

Osaka Bay

| Built up area |
| Higher ground |

0   5
km

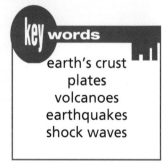

key words
earth's crust
plates
volcanoes
earthquakes
shock waves

Volcanic landscapes

A case study of Iceland

Iceland is the largest island on the North Atlantic Ridge. It is made entirely of volcanic materials. It is still growing as the Atlantic Ocean spreads and new volcanic material comes to the surface.

A **volcano** is where **lava**, **ash** and **gases** come to the surface. Some volcanoes erupt with a huge explosion. Others erupt slowly over a period of time.

The type of volcanic landscape depends on the kind of material that is erupted (see Figure 2).

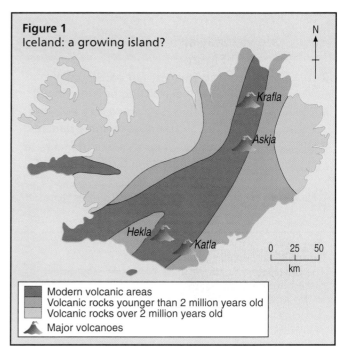

Figure 1
Iceland: a growing island?

N

Krafla

Askja

Hekla

Katla

0   25   50
km

Modern volcanic areas
Volcanic rocks younger than 2 million years old
Volcanic rocks over 2 million years old
Major volcanoes

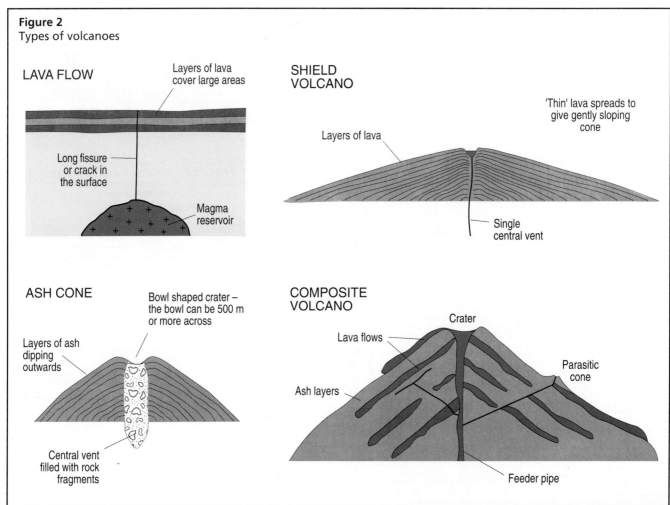

Figure 2
Types of volcanoes

LAVA FLOW

Layers of lava cover large areas

Long fissure or crack in the surface

Magma reservoir

SHIELD VOLCANO

'Thin' lava spreads to give gently sloping cone

Layers of lava

Single central vent

ASH CONE

Bowl shaped crater – the bowl can be 500 m or more across

Layers of ash dipping outwards

Central vent filled with rock fragments

COMPOSITE VOLCANO

Crater

Lava flows

Parasitic cone

Ash layers

Feeder pipe

1 Use an atlas map of the North Atlantic Ocean.

  a) Name the islands running along the middle of the Atlantic Ocean. They are virtually all volcanic islands.

  b) Look at Figure 1. How does it prove that Iceland is growing and spreading?

a)

Figure 3
Volcanoes on Iceland

b)

c)

d)

2 Study Figure 2 and the photographs in Figure 3.

Match the photographs to the types of volcanoes shown in Figure 2.

There are other kinds of volcanic activity as well as **volcanic eruptions**. Figures 4 and 5 show some of these.

Figure 4
Mud springs

Figure 5
Geyser

Figure 6
Fissure or crack caused by earthquakes as Iceland spreads to the east and west

Iceland is lacking in **natural resources**. Volcanic activity partly makes up for this. **Geothermal heat** is used to provide hot water and central heating. In Reykjavik, the capital city, whole districts of the city are heated by naturally hot water from boreholes. Greenhouses are also heated in this way. In the north of the island an electricity power station uses high pressure steam from deep boreholes.

key words

volcano
lava
ash
gases
volcanic eruption
natural resources
geothermal heat

25

2 TOURISM
Statistical maps and diagrams

unit 1

skills

Using maps and diagrams to get and give information.

In this unit you will see information about numbers, e.g. numbers of people, temperatures, hours of sunshine. This information is called **statistics**. It will be presented in tables and on maps.

Why do people go on holiday?

It will help if you spend a few minutes **brain storming** answers to this question. Write down reasons why people go on holiday and what they want from their holidays.

The graph in Figure 1 shows the time of year when people from the European Union (EU) take their holidays.

Figure 1
Holiday times of Europeans

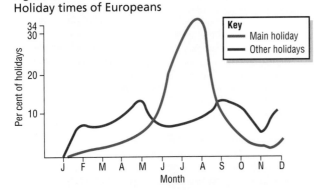

Key
— Main holiday
— Other holidays

1 a) What are the most popular months of the year for the main holidays?
  b) Give *two* reasons why you think these months are very popular?

The 'other holidays' on Figure 1 have three peak times of May, September/October and December.

2 What school holidays come at these times of the year?

Figure 2
Percentage of the population travelling abroad for holidays

Country	%	Country	%
Austria	41	Italy	16
Belgium	54	Luxemburg	62
Denmark	43	Netherlands	53
Finland	51	Norway	44
France	20	Portugal	13
Germany	35	Spain	14
Greece	14	Sweden	47
Iceland	37	Switzerland	54
Ireland	31	United Kingdom	18

The table in Figure 2 shows the percentage of people holidaying abroad from their home countries.

3 Use the information in Figure 2 to draw a bar graph.

4 Which country has the highest percentage of its population travelling abroad?

5 Look at the map of Europe in Figure 3. Why do you think the country you named in Question 4 has the highest percentage?

6 Complete this sentence by choosing the correct word in bold.
*The countries with the highest percentage of people holidaying abroad are in **Northern/Southern** Europe.*

7 Look back at your brain storming activity.
  a) Try to explain why your answer to Question 6 is true.

The map in Figure 4 shows where some of the British go on holiday. The width of the lines show the numbers of people travelling. You will need to measure the width and check it with the scale in the key to find the numbers.

Figure 3 Map of Europe

8 To which country do most visitors go?

9 Use the map scale to find out approximately how many visitors go to:
a) Greece;
b) Portugal;
c) Germany;
d) USA.

Did you think that the graphs and diagrams were easier to use than just tables of statistics?

Being able to read graphs and diagrams and answer the sort of questions you have seen in this unit is a useful skill. There are usually questions in exam papers using these skills and there are useful marks to be gained if you can answer them.

Figure 4
Where the British go on holiday

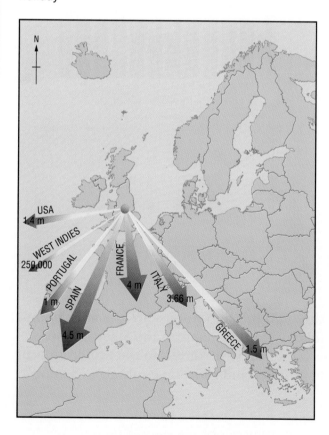

Figure 5

Figure 6

key words

statistics
brain storming

Mediterranean tourism

Why **Mediterranean** countries are so popular for holidays.

Before you start this unit, you will need to collect some brochures of Mediterranean holidays.

1 Look through the brochures. Make a list of the different countries that you find.

2 On Worksheet 2/2.2, colour in the holiday areas that you have just found.

You have probably coloured most of the countries of the Mediterranean. From time to time some countries are not used by tour operators.

3 Which countries have not been coloured? Can you think of reasons why they may not be popular?

Why is the Mediterranean a popular holiday destination – especially for the British?

Within Europe, July and August are the two most popular months for going on holiday.

Figure 1 shows the average temperatures, rainfall and sunshine for London in England and Benidorm in southern Spain.

4 Look at the information for July.
 a) How much hotter is Benidorm than London?
 b) How much wetter is London than Benidorm?
 c) Which place gets the most sunshine?
 d) How much more?

key word

Mediterranean

Figure 1
Average temperature, rainfall and sunshine hours for Benidorm and London

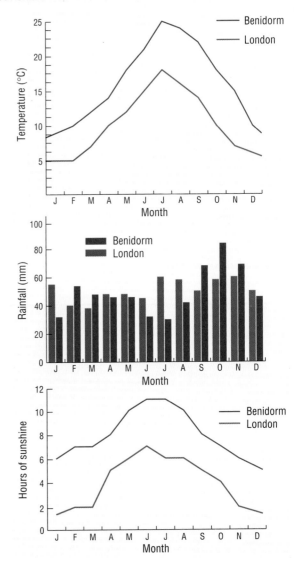

Although July and August are the most popular holiday months, many of the Spanish hotels stay open all year round. In the winter months many older and retired people go to Spain.

5 Look at Figure 1 again.
 a) Why might old people be tempted to to go to Spain in the winter?
 b) Why might they prefer winter to summer?

Figure 2
Resort, industry and agriculture

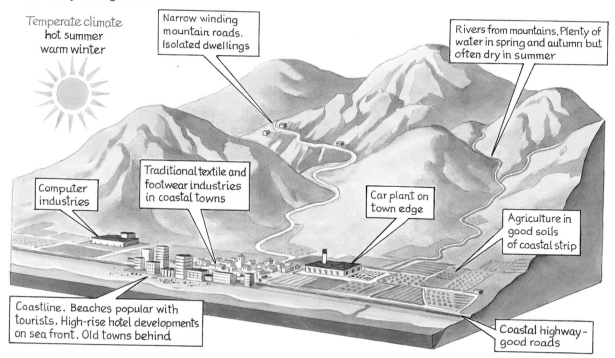

Temperate climate
hot summer
warm winter

Narrow winding
mountain roads.
Isolated dwellings

Rivers from mountains. Plenty of
water in spring and autumn but
often dry in summer

Computer
industries

Traditional textile and
footwear industries
in coastal towns

Car plant on
town edge

Agriculture in
good soils
of coastal strip

Coastline. Beaches popular with
tourists. High-rise hotel developments
on sea front. Old towns behind

Coastal highway -
good roads

Figure 3
Commune of Valencia

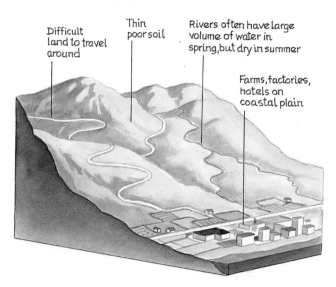

Difficult
land to travel
around

Thin
poor soil

Rivers often have large
volume of water in
spring, but dry in summer

Farms, factories,
hotels on
coastal plain

Spain was one of the earliest countries to benefit from large numbers of tourists. One region popular with tourists is the Commune of Valencia (see Figure 2).

The diagram in Figure 3 shows some things about the region.

During the peak holiday months, the population can rise to four times its normal number.

6 a) What part of the Valencia region do you think most people will visit?
   b) What time of year do you think the visitors arrive?

7 At what time of the year will the agricultural crops need irrigating?

8 The regional government want to build a water reservoir.
   a) On the diagram on Worksheet 2/2.2, mark with a cross where you think would be the best place to build the reservoir.
   b) Colour in blue the places on the diagram that will need to be supplied with water in the dry season.
   c) Draw an arrow to the places you have coloured and write down what the water will be used for (one has been done for you).

9 In the local paper, there have been some articles which have suggested that the Valencia region can do without the reservoir.

   Write a letter to the paper explaining why you think it will be needed.

Decision making

main idea

To show an example of a job needing geography skills

You have got a position in a local **travel agents** for work experience. The manager has asked you to put some brochures onto the shelves. Each section of shelf is labelled by the regional tourist boards. Figure 1 shows the names of the tourist boards.

One day a number of people come into the travel agents. You arrange with each of them their most suitable holiday. Unfortunately before you were able to file the information away, your notes were knocked onto the floor.

1 Complete the table on Worksheet 2/2.3 to show which holiday brochures go with each region.

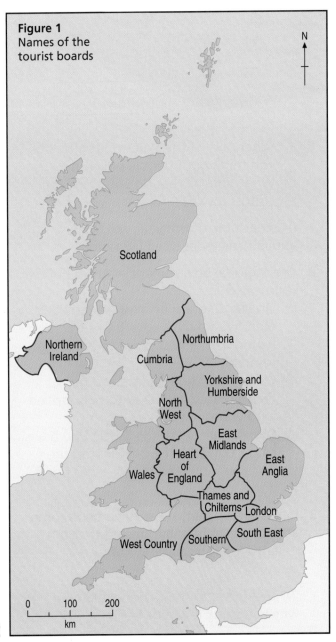

Figure 1 Names of the tourist boards

N

Scotland

Northern Ireland

Northumbria

Cumbria

Yorkshire and Humberside

North West

East Midlands

Heart of England

Wales

East Anglia

Thames and Chilterns

London

West Country

Southern

South East

0   100   200
km

Figure 2 Holidays for whom?

SEAVIEW HOTEL

Cruise the Med for 14 days
June 3rd – 17th

Visit Florida and Disneyland
Fun for all the family

See France by bike / 7 days
good hard cycling

Replace your energy with winter sun in Jamaica

TOURISM 2
unit 3

2 From Figure 2 and the following information, match the correct holidays to the various groups.

- Holiday A – Mediterranean Cruise
- Holiday B – Disney World Florida
- Holiday C – Cycling in France
- Holiday D – Winter sun

Figure 3
Travel brochure

RUSSIAN EXPERIENCE

Saturday: Cross from Dover to Calais, drive to Brussels for overnight stay.

Sunday: Drive to Germany to Hanover through Ruhr.

Monday: Drive to the capital city. Afternoon: sight-seeing tour includes Brandenburg gate and the remains of the wall.

Tuesday: Cross the River Oder and travel on to Warsaw, the capital city. Two nights stay at the Hotel Gromada.

Wednesday: Sight-seeing day, including morning guided tour and free afternoon for shopping.

Thursday: Cross the border into Russia and stop for lunch at Brest before continuing to Minsk for a sight-seeing drive before arriving at our hotel.

Friday: Leave Minsk and travel to Smolensk for lunch. After lunch travel to Moscow.

Saturday: Full sight-seeing day. Guided tour includes Red Square, Kremlin and St Basil's Cathedral. The afternoon is free for shopping and visiting the museums.

Sunday: leave for a scenic day's travel to Novgorad where we stay for the night.

Monday: After a morning tour of the city we travel to St Petersburg.

Tuesday: A full day's sight-seeing.

Wednesday: Leave St Petersburg and travel to Helsinki and travel overnight by ferry to Stockholm.

Thursday: Arrive in Stockholm in the morning and travel south to Helsingor and cross via ferry to Copenhagen.

Friday: After a morning's tour of the city, leave Copenhagen and cross the country to Rodbyhavn, where we cross by ferry into Germany. Bypass Hamburg and stay overnight in Bremen.

Saturday: A long day's travel along the motorways to reach Ostend for final overnight stop.

Sunday: Travel to Calais for the ferry to Dover.

Figure 3 shows details of a coach tour holiday of Northern Europe. You will need a copy of the map on the worksheet.

3 From the information in Figure 3, mark the route taken by the coach on your map.

4 a) What sea do you cross on the first day?
   b) What countries do you cross on Sunday?
   c) What is the capital city of Germany?
   d) Warsaw is the capital of which country?
   e) How many days are spent in Russia?
   f) In which country is Helsinki?
   g) What sea is crossed from Helsinki to Stockholm?

5 How many ferry crossings are made on this holiday?

6 Name all of the European Union countries that you travel through.

7 Imagine that you are lucky enough to win a large sum of money. You are going to plan a two week tour by car. It could be like the coach tour visiting several countries or it could just visit one country. Put together a brochure of your tour. You will need to decide:
- The order in which you visit each place.
- What you will do at each place e.g. swim and sunbathe, sight-see, visit museums and art galleries.
- Where you will stay.

8 Draw a map of your route.

9 For each place you visit, try to find a picture of it. Put the pictures in order and write underneath each one what you will do at that place. This is quite a big task but it should be good fun!

key word

travel agents

Theme park tourism

Factors influencing the siting of theme parks

Disneyland in the USA was probably the model for the theme parks in the United Kingdom.

There are a number of **leisure** parks or theme parks in this country. Some are simply very large fun fairs, e.g. Alton Towers, others recreate a period of history as a living museum e.g. the Black Country Museum in Dudley, West Midlands.

Whatever the idea of the parks, all of them rely on the public paying an entrance fee, in order to keep them going.

The choice you made should have been quite straightforward. People planning where to site parks will have to make choices which are not so easy.

What will they look for?

People are the most important factor to consider. Having people living within easy reach of a park means that there is more chance of attracting large numbers to the park.

This closeness does not just depend on distance, but also the ease of getting there (remember Getting to the Lake District in Book 1?). Some places have better accessibility than others.

Figure 1
Sites for a leisure park

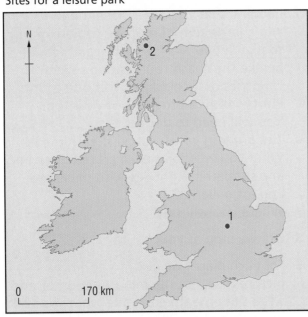

Figure 2
Alton Towers location

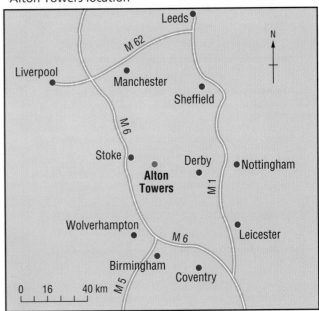

1 Figure 1 shows two possible **sites** for a leisure park.
   a) Which site would you choose to open a park?
   b) Try to give two reasons for your choice.

Parks may not be set up just because of the 'local' population but also because a large number of visitors will be drawn to the area by other attractions.

Historical Theme Parks need to be located within the area they are trying to recreate e.g. The Black Country Museum is in Dudley which is part of the Black Country.

As well as considering people, planners might choose sites which have been **reclaimed** from closed industries. The American Adventure Park in Derbyshire is built on an old open-cast mine and Beamish Open Air museum in County Durham is built on an old colliery.

You found out how to get to Alton Towers in Book 1. We will use Alton Towers to explore some of the ways in which its development has affected the local area.

Use Figures 2 and 3 to answer the following questions.

When you studied 'Getting to the Lake District' in Book 1 you saw that the motorways can lower the journey time.

3 Using an atlas find out which motorway(s) a driver would take to get to Alton Towers from the following:
   a) Durham;
   b) Bristol;
   c) London;
   d) Carlisle.

Figure 4
a) Old and new road near Alton Towers
b) Workers in Alton Towers c) Bed and breakfast

2 Using the major towns, how many people live:
   a) within 40 km of Alton Towers;
   b) within 80 km of Alton Towers?

4 Look at the photographs in Figure 4.
   a) What employment is there for local people?
   b) How has Alton Towers helped the local tourist trade?

Apart from Alton Towers, tourists are attracted to a nearby National Park.

5 What is the name of this National Park?

Figure 3
Population in the towns near Alton Towers

Place	Population (to the nearest '000)
Birmingham	1 025 000
Coventry	304 000
Derby	221 000
Leeds	455 000
Leicester	280 000
Liverpool	457 000
Manchester	742 000
Nottingham	278 000
Sheffield	528 000
Stoke	320 000
Walsall	179 000
Wolverhampton	247 000

key words
leisure
site
reclaim

Tourism and conservation

Tourism and conservation depend on each other.

National Parks in Kenya

Tourism is important to Kenya. It provides income from abroad which is needed to pay for imports. Tourism brings in nearly one-third of all foreign income.

There are beach resorts along the Indian Ocean coast. The major attraction of Kenya, however, is its **wildlife**.

Kenya has a large number of **National Parks**, National Reserves and Game Reserves.

In the National Parks wildlife has complete protection and human land use is not allowed.

On National Reserves and Game Reserves wildlife **conservation** comes first, but activities like cattle grazing are allowed.

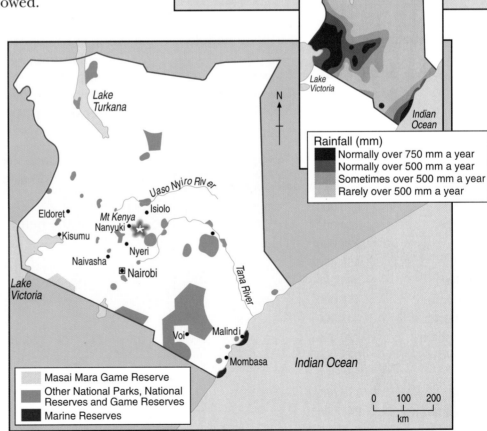

Figure 1
The location of Kenya

Rainfall (mm)
Normally over 750 mm a year
Normally over 500 mm a year
Sometimes over 500 mm a year
Rarely over 500 mm a year

Figure 2
National Parks and Reserves

Masai Mara Game Reserve
Other National Parks, National Reserves and Game Reserves
Marine Reserves

key words

tourism
wildlife
National Park
conservation

1 Look at Figure 2.
  a) How many parks and reserves are in the areas with more reliable rainfall (normally over 500 mm a year)?
  b) How many are in areas of less reliable rainfall?
  c) The largest is in an area of unreliable rainfall. Suggest two reasons for this.

The Masai Mara Game Reserve

There is a great variety of animal and bird life in this reserve. This makes it an attractive place for tourists. It has another advantage. It is only 160 km by road from Nairobi. For short safari holidays it is in a convenient location.

The inner part of the reserve is run like a National Park. There is no settlement there. In the rest the local Masai people are able to graze their cattle.

2 Use Figure 3 and the captions of the photographs in Figure 4.
  a) Why do areas have to be kept free from human use of the land?
  b) Why might some human usage of the land help the reserve?
  c) Why is the number of lodges and camp sites strictly controlled?
  d) Where does the name Masai Mara come from?

Figure 3
Masai Mara Game Reserve

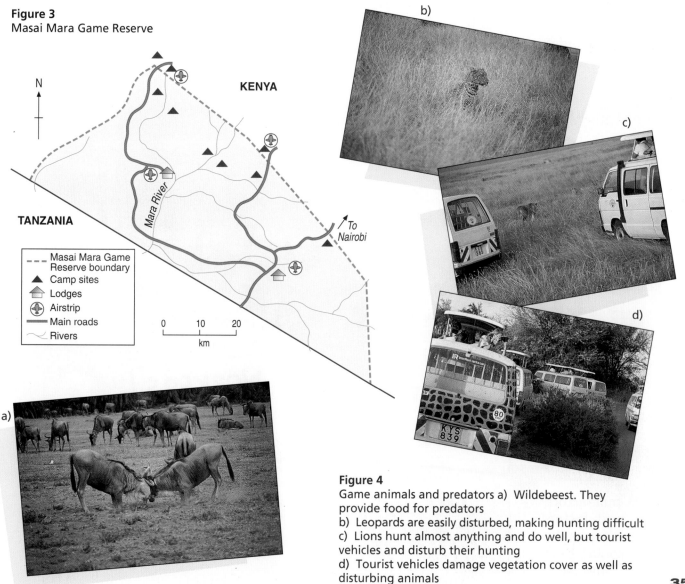

KENYA

N

TANZANIA

Mara River

To Nairobi

- - - Masai Mara Game Reserve boundary
▲ Camp sites
⌂ Lodges
✈ Airstrip
— Main roads
~ Rivers

0 10 20
km

a)
b)
c)
d)

Figure 4
Game animals and predators a) Wildebeest. They provide food for predators
b) Leopards are easily disturbed, making hunting difficult
c) Lions hunt almost anything and do well, but tourist vehicles and disturb their hunting
d) Tourist vehicles damage vegetation cover as well as disturbing animals

CITIES
Living in cities

City development has a pattern.

Most people live in a town or city. If you do not, then probably someone in your family or someone you know works there or you may go there to do your shopping.

How did towns and cities develop?

Most towns and cities grew up in the nineteenth century as people moved away from the countryside. People moved because they were **pulled** by jobs created by the Industrial Revolution and **pushed** from the countryside by the lack of jobs in farming.

This pattern of change, from living in small communities in the countryside, to living in towns is called **urbanisation**.

Some large towns are often referred to as cities. In some areas, the towns have grown so much that there is no rural land between them. They have joined together to form one large urban area which is called a **conurbation** (see Figure 2).

1 Use an outline map of the British Isles.
   a) Mark where you live with a dot.
   b) Which is the nearest conurbation to you? (If you live in one, which is the next nearest one?) Mark this on the map and label it.

Figure 1
Push and pull factors

NO WORKERS WANTED

PUSH FACTOR

WORKERS WANTED

PULL FACTOR

key words

pull factors
push factors
urbanisation
conurbation
model

Figure 2
Conurbations in Great Britain

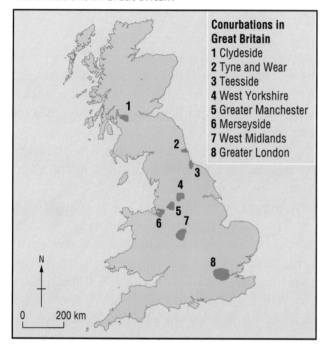

Complete the exercise on Worksheet 2/3.1. It shows how one city grew during the nineteenth and twentieth centuries.

Geographers have tried to explain the pattern of city growth using a **model**. It is unlikely that all cities exactly fit the model, but models do help to explain the general pattern of city developments.

Figure 3 shows a model of a city. Here is a description of each area shown on the model.

A The Central Business District (CBD). The main area of shops and offices.
B A mixture of Victorian terraced houses, industry and derelict land. In many cities some of this has been cleared and redeveloped.
C Better quality nineteenth century houses.
D Terraced/semi-detached houses.
E Old council estates.
F Modern council estates.
G Modern private housing.
H Expensive modern housing.
J Industrial estates.

2 The photographs in Figure 4 show examples of buildings in the model.
  a) Match the numbers on the model to the letters on the photographs.
  b) Try to draw a model of your town or city. Your teacher will show you how to do this. It is very unlikely that your model matches Figure 3 exactly.
  c) Does it have things in common? What are they?
  d) In what ways is your model different to Figure 3?

Figure 3
A city model

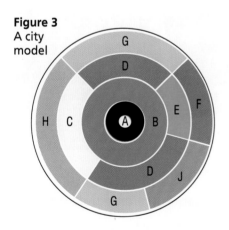

Figure 4
Types of building

Central Business Districts

main idea

> The location of the Central Business District and its role?

In Unit 1 of this chapter, the **Central Business District** was mentioned. It is usually referred to as the CBD – this is a lot less of a mouthful!

Where is the CBD and what is it?

The name gives us a clue as to where it is – central. The area is usually found in the heart of the town or city.

To find out what the CBD is, try this activity.

---

1 Make a list of reasons for going into your nearest town or city centre.

Include in the list reasons why your parents, relatives or neighbours go there.

If you need some help, look at the photographs in Figure 1 which show some of the activities that take place in a CBD.

In your list, you probably had examples of shopping, going to the bank or building society, visiting the library or the local council. Perhaps you suggested people worked in offices or visited theatres and cinemas. In the CBD there are:

- large department stores selling a wide range of goods, e.g. clothes, furniture, sports goods and electrical equipment;
- the principal department stores (e.g. Marks and Spencer, British Home Stores);
- specialist shops, e.g. selling books, clothes and jewellery etc;
- a large number of banks and building societies;
- a large number of the city's offices.

a)

. d)

Figure 1
a) Department store
b) Library
c) Theatre
d) Town Hall

b)

c)

---

2 Rewrite these sentences only putting in the correct word.

The rent for shops and offices will be <u>higher/lower</u> in the CBD than in other parts of the city.

This is because there is <u>more/less</u> demand for space.

One way to get more buildings on to a site is to build upwards. You are likely to see a large number of a city's tall buildings in the CBD.

For shopping, because there are often a number of shops selling the same sort of goods, the CBD offers the chance to compare the prices and quality of goods. It is probably here that people go to buy gifts and clothes or shoes for special occasions.

The CBD has, in most cases, grown up where routes into the city meet. These routes still exist and so there will be a lot of traffic in the area.

Figure 3
a) Roads closed to traffic

b) Enclosed shopping centre

3 Look at each of the people shown in Figure 2. Write down what they would like about each solution in Figure 3 and what they would dislike.

Figure 2
Conflicting needs of traffic and pedestrians

I don't want my son running around near cars

I need to park my van right next to the bank

I like to stop where it is dry and warm

I need to get my car close to the shops

There is a lot to draw people into the CBD and during the day there will also be a large number of pedestrians.

The needs of traffic and pedestrians can be in **conflict** with one another. Local planners have to try to keep both groups happy.

Figure 3 shows some solutions that towns and cities have found to deal with the difficulties.

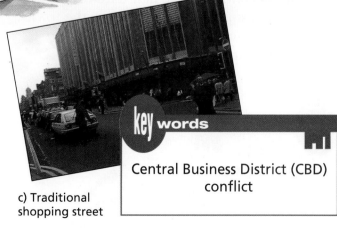

c) Traditional shopping street

key words

Central Business District (CBD)
conflict

Local and district shopping centres

main idea

There is only one city centre but there are many smaller shopping areas.

Figure 1
Outline of a city and its surrounding districts

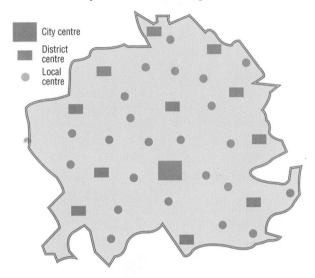

■ City centre
■ District centre
● Local centre

The outline of a city and its surrounding districts are shown in Figure 1. The various shopping areas found in a city or large town are marked on it. Shopping areas break down into the following parts.

- The corner shop is usually found in the older parts of town.
- The local shopping centre has perhaps 10 to 20 shops.
- Larger shopping centres, often called district shopping centres. Some may have been the centre of a small settlement before the town or city developed to swallow it up.
- The main shopping centre in the CBD.

key words

hierarchy
convenience foods
comparison shopping

Figure 2

a)

b)

c)

d)

1 Which shopping centre types are shown in Figure 2?

Figure 3
A shopping hierarchy

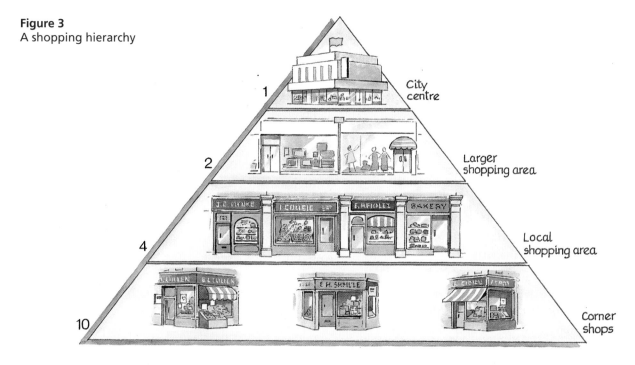

In a sports knockout competition there can only be one winner. Figure 3 shows that there is only one shopping centre.

In the same way, there is only one city centre, but there are many corner shops. There are fewer large shopping centres than there are local centres.

This is called a **hierarchy** of shopping areas.

> **2** What type of goods are bought in each of the shopping centres discussed above?

Here is a model answer:

- The corner shop is used by people for **convenience foods**, e.g. bread, milk, newspapers and perhaps items which have been forgotten when the main shopping was done.
- The local shopping centre is again used for convenience foods. It may have a small supermarket and will probably have some specialist shops such as a chemist and a post office.

- The larger shopping centre will probably have supermarkets, more specialist shops (e.g. a fish shop, sports shop, electrical goods shop). There may even be some opportunity for **comparison shopping**. These shopping areas are often on main routes into the city centre.
- The city centre is unlikely to have convenience goods shops. Unit 3 described the types of shop found in this area.

Worksheet 2/3.3 gives you the chance to see if your home town fits the model.

Did you find that the corner shop was used for convenience foods? Was there more choice of shops at the larger shopping centre than at the local one?

Your teacher may suggest some other things to explore with your results.

This hierarchy of shops has been with us for many years, but things are changing.

> **3** a) Why are corner shops closing down?
>   b) Why are there empty premises in town centres?

Unit 5 will give you more ideas on this question.

Industry

Over the years the location of industry has changes.

Industries can be grouped into three main types.

- **Primary** industries – where people take **raw materials** from the earth or sea, e.g. farming, fishing, forestry and mining.
- **Secondary** industries – the use of materials from primary industry to manufacture things, e.g. steel, furniture and textiles.
- **Tertiary** industries – these are professions which provide services, e.g. doctors, shop workers, lorry drivers.

Figure 1 shows some people doing different jobs.

The place where a factory or industry is placed is called its **location**. Primary industries have no choice where to locate. They have to be where the raw materials are.

In the past secondary industry was often **fixed** in its location. There were important reasons why it located where it did. In some cases the raw materials it used were heavy and expensive to transport so factories were set up near to the raw materials (see Figure 2). In other cases industry might have set up close to the market where it could sell its goods (see Figure 3).

---

1 Draw a table with three columns with the headings Primary, Secondary and Tertiary. Write down each of the jobs from Figure 1 in the correct column.

Figure 1
Different jobs

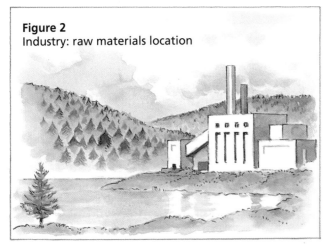

Figure 2
Industry: raw materials location

Figure 3
Industry: market location

In all cases the workforce would live near to the factories. This is why in the inner city, it is quite likely that you will find older industry mixed in with the older houses.

In Unit 1 of this chapter, you saw that inner city areas have often been redeveloped, with modern housing replacing the older terraced housing. Old factories which were usually large, may have been demolished and replaced with small industrial estates. Sometimes the factories remain but have been turned into smaller units (see Figure 4).

Figure 4
Old factory now occupied by a number of different firms

2 Why do you think industry no longer needs to be alongside the workers' houses?

There are still jobs in the middle of the city. Look at the jobs in Figure 6.

3 What type of industry do these fit into?

Figure 5
A factory

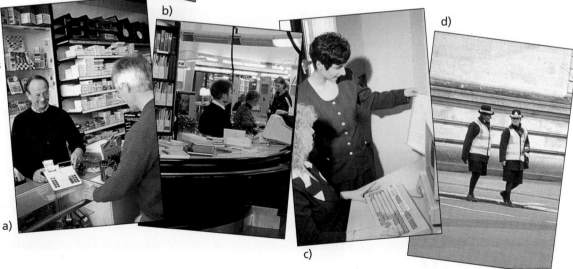

Figure 6
a) Shopworkers
b) Librarian
c) Office workers
d) Traffic warden

b)

d)

a)

c)

Some industries, from the 1930s onwards, have located along the main roads out of towns (Figure 5). Originally these would have been on **greenfield sites**. This means that when they were built the land was in the countryside just outside the town or city. However, as the city or town expanded these sites became part of the built up area.

With the difficulty of transport into urban areas, more industries are locating near to good road systems and out of the cities. They may find that land is cheaper here.

Today people travel to their work. This is called **commuting**. People going into the city will be mostly working in the tertiary industry. Many travelling out of the city will be working in the secondary industry.

key words

primary
raw materials
secondary
tertiary
location
fixed
greenfield site
commuting

New trends in services and industries

main idea

Secondary industry and retailers are moving away from their traditional locations.

Secondary industry

In the past, as we have seen, industry usually located in the inner city or in the suburbs.

Many industries today are **footloose**. This means that they do not need to locate near raw materials or near the market.

Often the raw materials and finished products are light and cheap to transport.

Figure 1
Industry location: site 1

Figure 2
Industry location: site 2

Figure 3
Modern
factory

1 Make a sketch of the factory shown in Figure 3. Underneath draw an arrow pointing to the factory. Now list all the pull reasons for moving here.

2 Now draw the factory in Figure 4. This time draw your arrow pointing away from the factory. List the reasons which might push the company away from here.

Figure 4
Old factory in
inner city

Some companies have moved from the inner cities to greenfield sites on the edge of towns. Other companies are new to an area and have chosen to locate on the edge of towns. What is the attraction of these sites, when there are often premises available in the towns themselves? Usually there are two sets of reasons:
• those that *push* the company from the town centres; and
• those that *pull* the company to the new sites.

Here are some push and pull reasons why a company might choose the site of Figure 1 rather than that of Figure 2.
• There is no room to expand.
• The site is close to major roads and a motorway.
• The buildings are old, cold and dark.
• The land is cheap to buy.
• Access to the factory is difficult.
• The factory and surroundings are pleasant to work in.

Shopping

Just like industry, some retailers have moved away from traditional town centre sites to purpose-built sites.

Sometimes these sites are built on the edge of towns like the industrial estates. Others are built on sites nearer the town centre that have been reclaimed from industry.

Most towns have at least one example of this type of site. Figure 5 shows one. Notice that the buildings look like small factories.

Figure 5
Retail park

Figure 7
All roads lead to Merry Hill

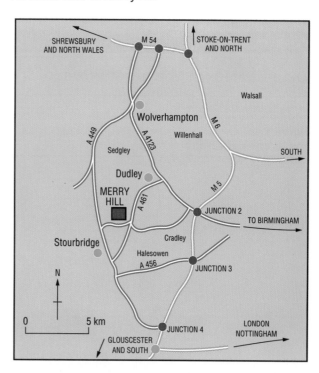

3 Why do you think these retailers in Figure 5 prefer this site to the town centre?

4 Use Figures 6 and 7 to help explain some of the reasons for Merry Hill's success. Look at the photograph in Figure 8.

5 What advantages does this site have over a CBD shopping centre for:
   a) a shopper;
   b) a delivery driver?

In the West Midlands a former steelworks now houses the Merry Hill shopping centre on a 50 ha site. It is the second largest retail complex in the country and attracts a large number of shoppers each day.

Not everybody sees these **out-of-town shopping centres** as a good idea.

Figure 6
Number of people living within 5 minute's and 1 hour's drive from Merry Hill

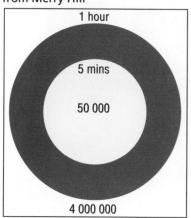

1 hour

5 mins

50 000

4 000 000

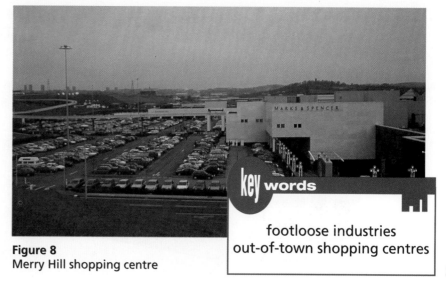

Figure 8
Merry Hill shopping centre

key words

footloose industries
out-of-town shopping centres

45

Renewing a city area

---

main idea

Derelict areas can be transformed.

Figure 1
The location of Cardiff

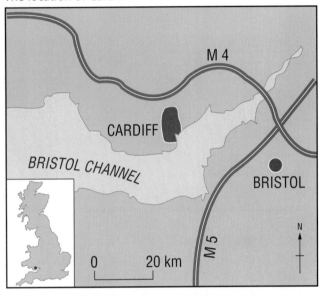

Figure 2
Cardiff Civic
Centre

Figure 3
Shopping
centre

Cardiff is the **capital city** of Wales. It is on the south coast of Wales where the River Severn enters the Bristol Channel.

Cardiff grew because of its development as a port to export coal from the South Wales valleys.

The port, once the world's largest coal exporter, is run down and, until recently, so was the surrounding area (see Figures 4 and 5).

In 1987 The Welsh Office decided to improve the area. They set up the Cardiff Bay Development Corporation (CBDC) whose role was to:
- improve the environment;
- attract new industry;
- develop new housing.

Although the Government gave some financial help, the CBDC had to attract investment from private industry.

Figure 4
Run
down
dockland
area

Figure 5
Area for
redevelopment

Figure 6
Cardiff Bay at low water

Figure 7
Cardiff Bay at high water

1 Look at Figure 6. What disadvantage can you see in attracting residents to the areas?

The difference between high and low water at Cardiff is large (14 m). Figure 7 is a photograph taken at high tide from the same place as Figure 6. Which view is more likely to attract people to the area?

In order to always have a high water level in the bay, the CBDC is building a **barrage** or dam across Cardiff Bay. The water coming down the Rivers Taff and Ely will not be able to flow into the sea and it will create a lake.

The people in Figure 8 have different views about building a barrage.

2 Imagine you are a reporter for the South Wales Echo. Use the information from Figure 8 to write an article about the barrage. Try to be fair and give both sides of the argument.
3 The photographs in Figure 9 on the worksheet were taken in different parts of the area. Use the information given on the worksheet to identify where they were taken.

A plan of the whole redevelopment scheme is shown on Worksheet 2/3.6.

Figure 8 Building a barrage

Where will the pollution from the rivers go when the barrier is built?

I'll be able to get to my yacht at any time

Waterside offices will create jobs for Cardiff people

Why don't they use the barrier to help create electricity?

Where will all the birds go when the mud flats disappear?

key words

capital city
barrage

Coping with urban change

main idea

Towns change over time.

Swindon is the largest **settlement** in Wiltshire but the county town is Trowbridge.

If you live in a town and your family have lived there all their lives (especially your grandparents) they will probably tell you the place has changed since they were young.

Some places change more than others. Swindon has changed in many ways.

The original settlement was in Old Town, where a village grew up around the manor house. The area relied on farming for its livelihood.

> **1** Work out the sort of animals that were farmed in the area. The clue is in the old name for the town, Swine Down.

The old town of Swindon did not change greatly until the middle of the nineteenth century. It was then that the Great Western Railway was built, joining London to Bristol. It was decided to build the engine works at Swindon.

Look at the route of the railway line between London and Bristol in Figure 1.

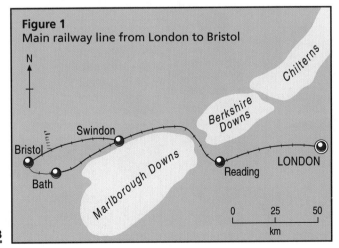

Figure 1
Main railway line from London to Bristol

N

Bristol
Bath
Swindon
Marlborough Downs
Berkshire Downs
Chilterns
Reading
LONDON

0   25   50
km

> **2** Why do you think the railway did not take a more direct route between London and Bristol?

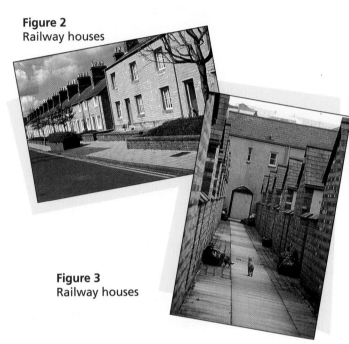

Figure 2
Railway houses

Figure 3
Railway houses

Old Swindon is on a hill about 1.5 km from where the railway passed. The railway company built houses for its workers near to the railway works (see Figures 2 and 3) and the settlement expanded around it. Even now this expanded area of Swindon is called New Town.

In 1900 Old Town and New Town became one town – the largest in Wiltshire.

The present town centre of Swindon is on the edge of New Town.

> **3** Look at the photographs of Old Town and New Town in Figures 4 and 5. Write a couple of sentences comparing the two shopping areas.

Swindon grew again after the 1939–45 war. There was a need to relieve **overcrowding** in London. New housing estates were built on the edge of the town.

From the 1970s, the railway works were in **decline**. They are now closed.

Unlike other towns that relied mainly on one industry, Swindon has not declined. It has continued to expand with factories, offices and housing all being built.

4 What relatively recent transport development has helped Swindon to expand?

Figure 4
Old Town shopping

Figure 5
New Town shopping

Figure 6
Map of Swindon

key words
settlement
overcrowding
decline
footloose industries

5 Imagine you work for a Swindon estate agent. Two customers have asked you to find them a site where they can set up their businesses. Retail development has to take place on retail land and industry on industrial land. The two customers are:
a) a large superstore (e.g. Sainsbury, Tesco etc);
b) A company making computer spare parts. They say they will deliver anywhere in the UK within 24 hours.

State where you will site each company and why you have chosen each site (use the information from Unit 6 of this chapter to help you).

Swindon has been able to attract **footloose industries** to the town (see Chapter 3, Unit 6) and it has a large number of industries linked to micro-electronics (see Chapter 4, Unit 8).

The land use is shown in Figure 6.

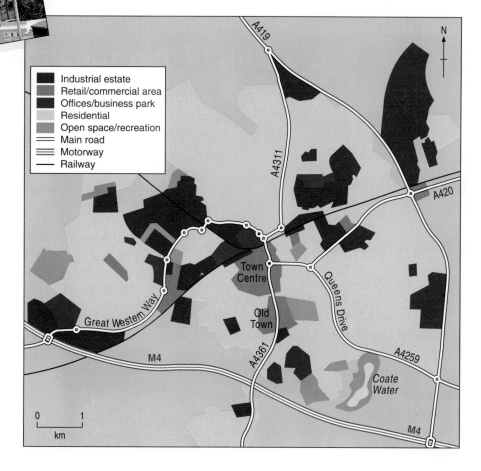

Chapter 3 unit 8

Population changes

main idea

> Population patterns change.

People move about. They move house, perhaps to another town, another part of the country or even to a different country.

1 Make a list of reasons why you think people might want to move.

In most parts of the United Kingdom the **census** shows a changing population. In general, big cities are losing people and small towns are gaining people.

Figure 1 is a diagram showing the kinds of changes which have been going on over the last 30 years.

Figure 1
Model of population change

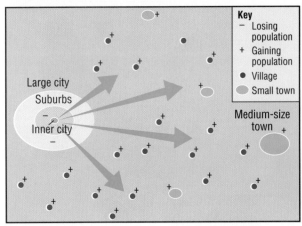

2 Look at Figure 1. In which kind of place do you live? Have you or your parents noticed any changes in the numbers of people?

Look at the map of the West Midlands on Worksheet 2/3.8. It shows local authority districts. Figure 2 gives their **population changes**.

Figure 2
West Midlands: population change, 1981–1991

District	Population Change (%)
Hereford and Worcester	
1 Bromsgrove	2.82
2 Hereford	5.02
3 Leominster	5.66
4 Malvern Hills	6.94
5 Redditch	16.07
6 South Herefordshire	8.92
7 Worcester	7.29
8 Wychavon	6.93
9 Wyre Forest	2.43
Shropshire	
10 Bridgnorth	−1.03
11 North Shropshire	4.93
12 Oswestry	9.98
13 Shrewsbury and Atcham	4.72
14 South Shropshire	12.26
15 The Wrekin	11.82
Staffordshire	
16 Cannock Chase	3.66
17 East Staffordshire	1.56
18 Lichfield	3.04
19 Newcastle-under-Lyme	−0.12
20 South Staffordshire	7.86
21 Stafford	0.56
22 Staffordshire Moorlands	−1.60
23 Stoke-on-Trent	−3.20
24 Tamworth	7.39
Warwickshire	
25 North Warwickshire	0.36
26 Nuneaton and Bedworth	1.90
27 Rugby	−2.93
28 Stratford-on-Avon	3.93
29 Warwick	1.78
West Midlands	
30 Birmingham	−6.86
31 Coventry	−6.08
32 Dudley	0.50
33 Sandwell	−7.26
34 Solihull	−1.42
35 Walsall	−3.81
36 Wolverhampton	−5.20

50

3 Use a blank copy of the worksheet map and the statistics in Figure 2.
  a) Colour in red the districts gaining people.
  b) Colour in blue the districts losing people.
  c) How does the result compare with Figure 1?

Figure 3
a) Conurbation b) Derelict inner city land c) Small town industrial estate d) Country town centre e) Road traffic in city f) Open roads in the country

4 The photographs in Figure 3 match the different kinds of area shown in Figure 1 and the worksheet map. Their locations are shown by numbers on the map.
  a) Match the photograph letter to the numbers. Write the letters on the map you used for Question 3.
  b) Choose one of the photographs. Put yourself in the position of one of the following people. Say what they think about the area.
    • Local resident;
    • property developer;
    • industrialist;
    • commuter.
  c) Why do you think there has been a movement of people from the big cities to smaller towns?

key words
census
population change

Fieldwork in towns

skills

main ideas

a) Carrying out a traffic survey;
b) working out the sphere of influence.

Perhaps you have already been out and tested some of the ideas suggested in other units of this chapter.

This unit is going to suggest two other areas that can be explored.

Carrying out a traffic survey

One of the problems in most towns is transport. Cars, buses and lorries end up sitting in traffic queues, especially in rush hours.

If local authorities are to prevent traffic jams, they need evidence of where the problems are.

One way of finding this out is to conduct a **traffic survey**. You can find out which sorts of vehicles use the roads. Figure 1 shows one way in which you can record this.

As each vehicle passes, a mark is made on the tally count. At the end of the activity, the tally count is totalled and the end column completed. From the figures in the table, a bar chart (see Figure 2) can be drawn.

Figure 2 Bar chart showing vehicles at Shannon Road

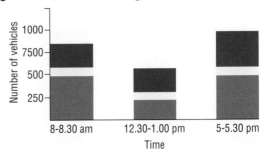

1 Which type of vehicle uses Shannon Road most:
   a) in the morning;
   b) at mid-day;
   c) in the evening?

Figure 1 Traffic survey

Name: *Janet Evans*   **Location:** *Shannon Road*

Time: *5–5.30 pm*

Cars					Total
✓	✓	✓	✓	✓	
✓	✓	✓	✓	✓	
✓	✓	✓	✓	✓	
✓	✓	✓	✓	✓	
✓	✓	✓			

Vans/Lorries					Total
✓	✓	✓	✓	✓	
✓	✓	✓	✓	✓	
✓	✓	✓			

Cycles/Motor cycles					Total
✓	✓	✓	✓	✓	
✓					

key words

traffic survey
sphere of influence

The council may want to know the total number of vehicles travelling on a road system. A possible trouble spot is shown in Figure 3. The numbers on the map show the points where traffic counts were carried out.

These were the counts at each of the points.

1	300	6	200
2	300	7	700
3	100	8	200
4	50	9	500
5	300	10	250

Figure 3
Traffic count sites

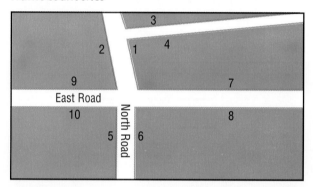

Figure 4
Traffic flow

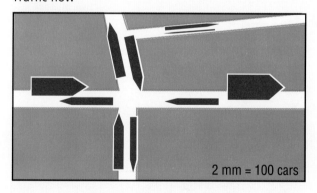

2 mm = 100 cars

In Figure 4 arrows have been drawn to represent these figures. Each arrow is drawn so that 2 mm represents 100 vehicles.

2 Complete this statement.

'If I was planning to put traffic lights at the cross-roads I would give <u>more/less</u> time to the East road than to the North road because _____'

Spheres of influence

Think about these issues.

- How important is your town to its region?
- Does your town influence people who live some distance away from it? What is this distance?

These questions can be tackled in a number of ways. For example, if the town has an evening newspaper, how far away from the town is it delivered?

Figure 5
Where the Nottingham Evening Post is sold

Figure 6
Nottingham telephone book area

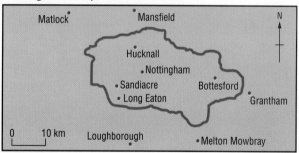

Figure 5 shows the area around Nottingham where the evening newspaper, the *Nottingham Evening Post* is delivered. Figure 6 shows the area covered by the Nottingham telephone directory. The area covered is called the **sphere of influence** of the town.

There are other ways to measure the sphere of influence. If your town has shops which deliver to customers, check how far away they deliver. Do the pupils in your school travel from a wide area? If they do then you could draw a map to show the sphere of influence of the school.

CHANGING GEOGRAPHY
Problem solving

main idea

Geography deals with many different tasks.

Using transport systems

Figure 1
Hong Kong's
Mass Transit
Railway (MTR

1 Look at the **map** of Hong Kong's Mass Transit Railway (MTR) and Kowloon-Canton Railway (KTR) in Figure 1.

You start from Central station.
- You want to travel by the shortest route to Lam Tin station. Where will you change trains?
- Name the station where you can change to the Kowloon-Canton Railway.
- You want to return via Jordan. Which lines do you take and where do you change lines?

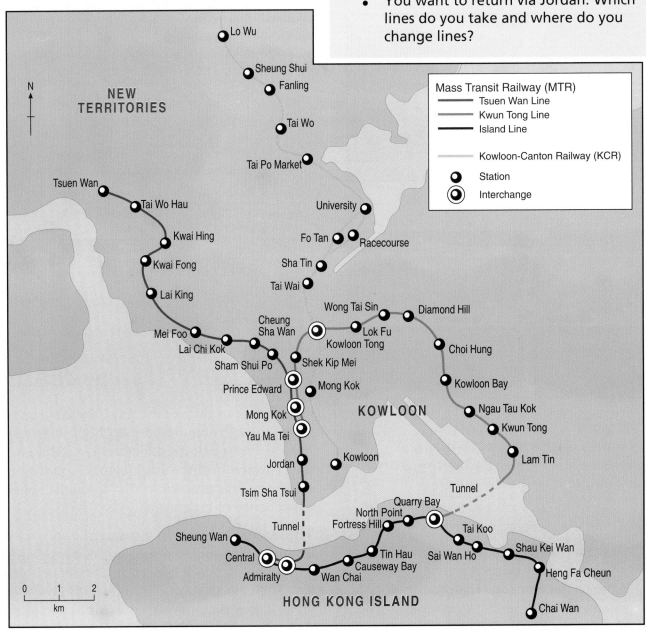

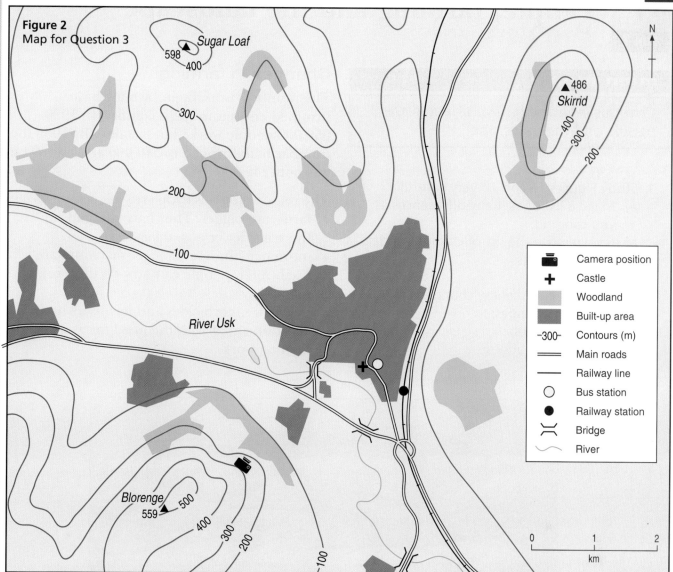

Figure 2
Map for Question 3

Identifying features on maps and photographs

Figure 3 Abergavenny

2 Look at Figures 2 and 3. You also need to use the sketch of the **photograph** on Worksheet 2/4.1.
a) In which direction was the camera pointing?
b) Write the following labels in the correct boxes on your sketch:
- River Usk;
- town centre;
- Skirrid;
- wood;
- Sugar Loaf;
- railway line;
- hospital;
- castle.

key words

map
photographs

People, farming and the landscape

1 Study Figures 1a and 1b very carefully.
   a) Make a list of as many differences as you can find.
   b) Now rewrite the list of changes under these headings:
      Farm changes;
      Landscape or scenery changes;
      Transport changes;
      People changes;
      Settlement changes.

Changes in farming

The numbers working in **farming** have dropped enormously this century. In 1930 850 000 people worked in farming. By 1965 the number had dropped to 510 000 and by 1994 it was only 242 000.

The reasons for this drop are:
- farms are bigger. They have merged, so there are fewer actual farmers;
- more machines and bigger machines are used. A few people can now do the work of many;
- pesticides, herbicides and fertilisers have also done away with the need for as much manual work.

Figure 1
Changes in the countryside

a/ 50 years ago

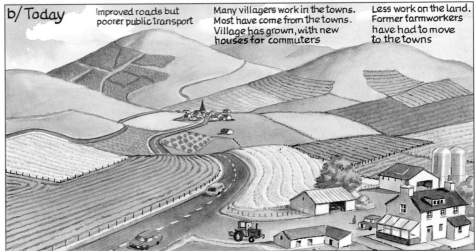

b/ Today

Improved roads but poorer public transport

Many villagers work in the towns. Most have come from the towns. Village has grown, with new houses for commuters

Less work on the land. Former farmworkers have had to move to the towns

key words

farming
landscape

Changing landscapes

The changes in farming and other areas have had a big effect on the **landscape**.

Figure 2
The countryside is changing

Changing life

The cartoons in Figure 2 show some of the changes and their effects.

2 Look at the cartoons and the box of possible sentences for the empty speech bubbles in Figures 2 and 3.

Use your own copies of the cartoons and complete the empty speech bubbles.

3 Put yourself in the position of someone of your age living in the countryside.

EITHER imagine you belong to a family which has moved there from a big town, OR imagine your family has lived there always.

Write a short letter to your local newspaper saying what you think of the place and the problems you have.

Figure 3
Speech bubbles

Use these for the speech bubbles. You can put some together.

1 There is little chance of work in the countryside.
2 If you are unemployed it is difficult to get to the places that have jobs.
3 Houses which were once tied to the jobs have been sold to people from the cities.
4 Younger people have moved to cities.
5 Local shops have closed because the new people drive to the city to shop.
6 Public transport gets worse or else disappears altogether.
7 The people moving in are wealthier and they push up the price of houses.
8 With fewer people there are fewer children and so schools are forced to close.
9 Outsiders object to changes which might bring in work but will spoil the look of the village.

People and villages

Villages are old settlements and some people prefer them to remain unchanged.

Patterns of settlement

In rural areas there are two sorts of settlement:

- **nucleated** settlements (villages and hamlets);
- **dispersed** settlements (farms and other single houses).

Figure 1
a) Village b) Farm

Figure 2
Pattern of settlements in the Vale of Glamorgan

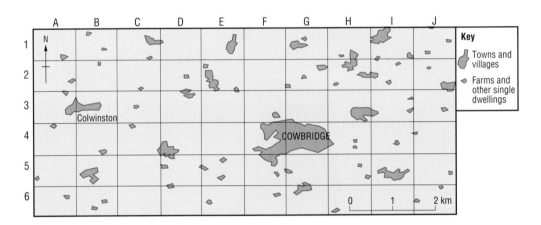

Key
🔸 Towns and villages
🔹 Farms and other single dwellings

Colwinston

COWBRIDGE

0   1   2 km

Figure 3
Patterns of settlement
a) Clustered
b) Random spread
c) Regular spread

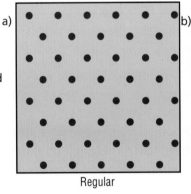
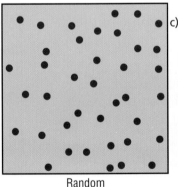
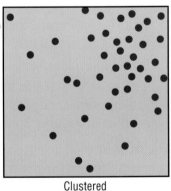

a)   b)   c)

Regular   Random   Clustered

1 a) Look at Figure 2. Using place names or the map's reference system, give an example of:
   - a nucleated settlement;
   - a dispersed settlement.
   b) Look at Figure 3. Which **pattern** is most like the map of the Vale of Glamorgan?

A changing village

Villages were originally rural communities. Many people worked on farms. The village itself would have had a number of shops as well as a school. Times have changed. Now, few people work on farms. Many people in the village have moved there from nearby towns and cities.

2 Study Figure 4.
 a) Where is the original part of the village?
 b) Which are the newer parts?
 c) What are the **functions** of this village?
 d) What **changes** seem to have taken place?
 e) Where are people likely to work?
 f) How are they likely to travel to work?

3 Suppose there was a plan to build a small factory on the edge of the village. People in the village would probably have different **views** about it.
 a) Why might some people support the idea?
 b) Why might some people be against it?
 c) Put yourself in the place of a reporter for the local newspaper. Write a short article about what villagers think. Your editor has already done the headline (see Figure 5).

Figure 4
The village plan: a) Village pub b) New house c) Church d) Post office e) Renovated older house f) Village school g) Farm

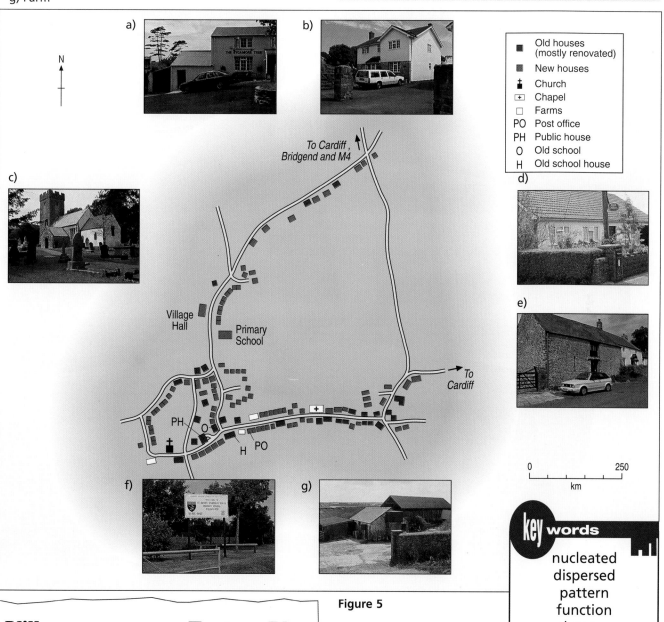

Figure 5

Villagers row over Factory Plan

key words
nucleated
dispersed
pattern
function
changes
views

Land use on the city edge

Is the land on the edges of cities still used for farming?

Changes on the edges of the cities

On the edges of the cities farming still goes on, but there are lots of **changes**. There are other ways to use the land.

Figure 1

a)
b)
c)
d)
e)
f)

key words

changes
conurbation
green belt
land use

a) Riding school (2007);
b) Sports club (2001);
c) Cricket field (1202);
d) Archery field (2101);
e) Golf course (1706);
f) Trout fishing pool (1308);

Look at the set of photographs in Figure 1 which were taken from the edge of a **conurbation**. The area is actually classed as a **green belt**. This means that **land use** is controlled to preserve the rural character of the area.

In other areas there are more developments such as industrial buildings and warehouses, new roads and motorways. In villages and towns near major conurbations, estates of new houses have shot up.

1 Use a copy of the diagram on Worksheet 2/4.4.
  a) Mark the locations of each of the photographs (the grid references are given in the captions).
  b) Which ones do you think show changes of land use?
  c) Do you think these changes are good or not? Give some reasons for your view.

g) New house (1906);
h) Garden centre (1209);
i) Farmland (1510);
j) School (2009);
k) Cemetery (1804);
l) Country park (1106)

main idea

Type of farm depends on many factors.

Figure 1
Farmer's decisions

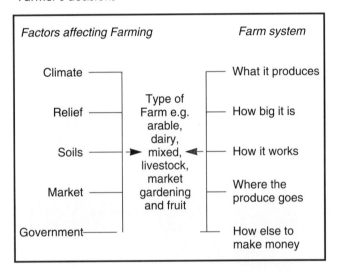

Hazel Brow Farm in the Yorkshire Dales

The Yorkshire Dales is a mountainous area in the north of England. Rainfall is heavy. Temperatures are cooler than in lowland areas. Summers are too short and too cool for anything except grass to grow well.

The **natural environment** sets limits to what farmers can do. Here, animal rearing is the only real option.

Hazel Brow Farm is in a National Park. This means there are **restrictions** on what can be done to the buildings. They have to fit in with the traditional building materials. Grants are available but they would mean making changes to the **farm system**.

This is mainly a sheep farm, but it also has a herd of dairy cattle. This brings a steady income from milk sales as well as from calves sold for beef. Some pigs are also reared. Other **income** comes from tourists.

1 Look at Figure 1. Copy and complete the passage using these words:

mixed farms; arable; flowers and vegetables; cattle for beef or milk; orchard; pigs; sheep.

'Farmers growing crops are involved in _____ farming. Livestock farming covers the rearing of animals such as, _____ _____, _____, _____. Farmers who grow crops and rear animals have _____ _____. Fruit farming includes _____ crops. Horticulture or market gardening includes the growing of _____ _____ __ _____, often under glass.'

The **type of farm** depends on what the area is like. Generally, a farmer chooses the most profitable activity for that area.

2 Use Figure 2 to answer these questions about the farm.
   a) How much land is there?
   b) How is it used?
   c) What affects its use?
   d) What type of farm is it?
   e) How many people work on the farm?
   f) What brings in money?
   g) Why do you think a variety of income sources is needed?
3 Copy and complete Figure 3. This is a diagram showing the farm system. It is a way of showing how the farm works.

key words

type of farm
natural environment
restrictions
farm system
income

Figure 2
A farm in the Yorkshire Dales

Relief
- Flat land on valley bottom
- Steep valley sides
- High pasture and moorland

Animals
- 380 sheep (lambing ewes) and
- 17 rams
- 70 pigs
- 37 cows (27 milkers and heifers)
- calves

a) Swaledale

Size
- 80ha (larger than average for the area)
- Fragmented (separate pieces of land; extra land bought)

Buildings and equipment
- Barns for lambing and keeping cattle in winter
- Milking parlour
- Tractors, etc

b) Machinery

Yorkshire Dales

c) Dairy Barn

d) Lambing pen

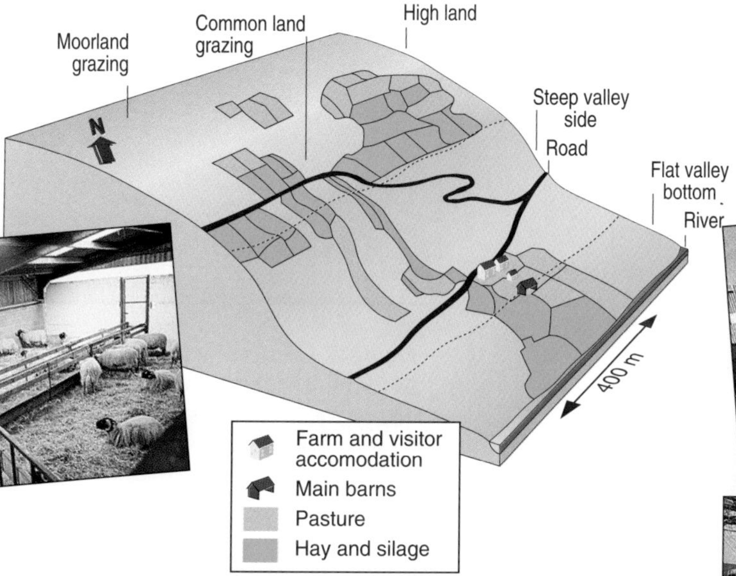

Moorland grazing
Common land grazing
High land
Steep valley side
Road
N
Flat valley bottom
River
400 m

Farm and visitor accomodation
Main barns
Pasture
Hay and silage

e) Barns

g) Self-catering accommodation

h) Spring time

Income
- Sale of lambs
- Sale of wool (very small income)
- Sale of pigs
- Sale of milk
- Sale of calves
- Farm visits and visitors in groups or individually
- Holiday accomodation – 2 self-catering properties
- National Park for barn repairs

f) Dairy parlour

Land use
- Pasture for sheep all year; dairy cattle in summer
- Hay and silage to feed animals, especially in winter
- Grazing on common land
- Grazing on moorland

Workers
- 4 (2 couples) plus
- Occasional extra help
- Contractors cut silage and hay

Figure 3
The farm system

Income

Grant from ____ ____ to repair ____.

The Farm

____ ha

Valley bottom to ____ ____ ____ and _____ and ____

Sheep, pigs, ____ , calves

Hay and _____, pasture, grazing on ____ ____ and

Holiday accomodation

Labour (__)

Buildings (e.g. ____)

Equipment (e.g. ____)

Lambs and ____

____ and calves

Income

Pigs

Visitors

Profit

Farming patterns

main idea

The pattern of farming is affected by physical and human factors.

The Vale of Evesham

The Vale of Evesham is a well-known **market gardening** area (Figure 1).

Figure 1
Location of the Vale of Evesham

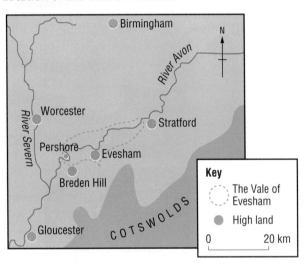

Key
- ⬭ The Vale of Evesham
- 🔴 High land
0   20 km

Physical factors are important in the growth of market gardening in the Vale of Evesham (Figures 2 and 3).

Figure 3
The coming of spring and length of growing season

In the Vale of Evesham spring starts early and the growing season lasts longer than in other places nearby

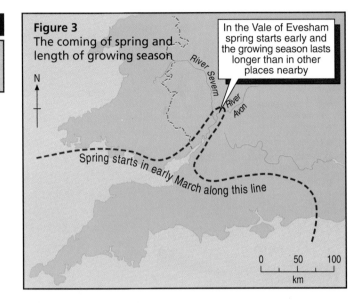

Spring starts in early March along this line

0   50   100
km

Figure 4 Physical factors and market gardening in the Vale of Evesham

Physical factor	Relevance to market gardening
Early spring	
Terraces	
Slopes	
Soils	

1 Look at Figures 2 and 3. Make a copy of Figure 4.

   Write the labels from Figures 2 and 3 in the correct boxes on Figure 4.

Figure 2
Cross-section through the Vale of Evesham

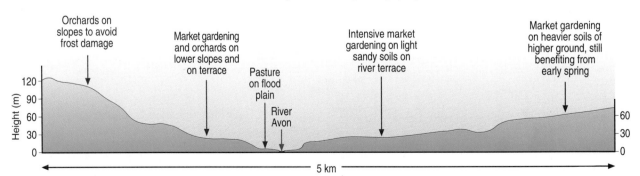

The whole area gains from having an early spring

Orchards on slopes to avoid frost damage

Market gardening and orchards on lower slopes and on terrace

Pasture on flood plain

River Avon

Intensive market gardening on light sandy soils on river terrace

Market gardening on heavier soils of higher ground, still benefiting from early spring

Height (m)

← 5 km →

This is an area of **intensive cultivation**. A great deal of work is done on the land and every bit of land is used. This means that the farmers or smallholders can get two, three or even more crops from their land.

Human factors are as important in the Vale of Evesham as physical ones.

- Much of the land in the Vale of Evesham is divided into **smallholdings**. To make a living farmers have to cultivate it intensively. They must also grow high value crops. Fresh fruit, vegetables and flowers are high value crops.
- The farmers' **co-operatives** buy goods in bulk and sell their produce together. This gives them the advantages of a central system of selling and transport.
- The area is near to the Midlands which is a major **market** for the produce. Motorways (and railways in the past) allow rapid transport of fresh produce to markets.

Figure 5
Intensive cultivation with land divided into strips for different crops with cloches to speed up growth; glasshouses allow all year cultivation

Figure 6

Glasshouse cultivation with heating plant

2 Look at the photographs in Figures 5 and 6.
List all the ways that tell you that the land is being cultivated intensively.

3 Make a copy of Figure 7. Complete the labelling using words from the last three paragraphs.

Figure 7 Human factors and market gardening in the Vale of Evesham

1 Smallholdings
To make a living farmers:
a) need to practise _____ _____ to get more than one crop a year;
b) have to grow high value crops like _____ _____, _____ and _____.

↓

Successful

market

gardening

2 Co-operatives
Allow farmers to:
a) buy goods in _____;
b) _____ produce together;
c) save on _____ costs.

3 Markets
a) Easy access to markets in the _____, South Wales and London;
b) Rapid transport using _____ in the past and _____ today.

 **words**

market gardening
physical factors
intensive cultivation
human factors
smallholdings
co-operatives
market

Patterns of land use

Patterns of farming can be seen at a national scale.

Denmark

Denmark is well-known for dairy production. It exports butter, bacon, eggs and fresh, frozen and canned foods based on cattle, pigs and poultry.

The country decided to practise **intensive** dairy farming. It is a small country and this was the best way to get a high income. Denmark is located close to the big industrial countries of Europe like Germany and Britain. They provide a nearby market for Denmark's produce.

Most land is used for growing crops (see Figure 1). It is **arable** land. The reason for this is that 85 per cent of the crops are used for animal **fodder**. Very little land is used for permanent pasture.

Figure 1
Land use map of Denmark

Mainly sandy soils

SWEDEN

Mainly clay soils

JUTLAND

D E N M A R K

SJAELLAND

FUNEN

FALSTER

LOLLAND

0   50   100
km

GERMANY

Main crops are rye, oats and potatoes. Farms are less intensive than in the east. Many areas are covered by coniferous plantations

Area of intensive farming. Farm yields are 20% more than in the west. Main crops are barley, wheat, sugar beet, market gardening and orchards

Figure 2
Farming in Denmark

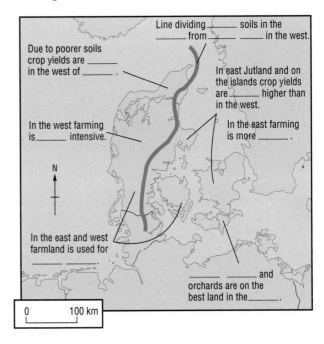

Line dividing _____ soils in the _____ from _____ _____ in the west.

Due to poorer soils crop yields are _____ in the west of _____ .

In east Jutland and on the islands crop yields are _____ higher than in the west.

In the west farming is _____ intensive.

In the east farming is more _____ .

N

In the east and west farmland is used for _____ _____ .

_____ _____ and orchards are on the best land in the _____ .

0   100 km

Figure 3
Land use

Land use	%
Grain crops (wheat, rye, barley, oats)	56
Rotation grass	14
Pulses and root crops	22
Permanent grass	8

Differences in physical geography have affected the pattern of land use (see Figure 3).

- Poor sandy soils are in the west. They cannot be farmed as intensively as the clay soils.
- The best land is in the east. This is where market gardening and orchards are found.

1 Use a copy of Figure 2. Complete the labelling and add a label to the blank arrow. Add at least one label of your own.

Western Australia

Most of western Australia is desert or semi-desert. The south west of the state, though, has a Mediterranean type climate (hot, dry summers and warm, wet winters).

2 Compare the map of farming types with the map of rainfall in Figures 4 and 5.
  a) How does the rainfall change from south west to north east?
  b) How do farming types change from the south west towards the north east?
  c) What is the most important **factor** affecting the types of farming?
  d) Fruit and dairying are both found in the Perth area where most people in south west Australia live. Write a sentence using the word *market* to explain this.

3 In Denmark and western Australia farming has been affected by **human factors** and **physical factors**. Make a list of those factors.

Figure 4
Farming types in south west Australia

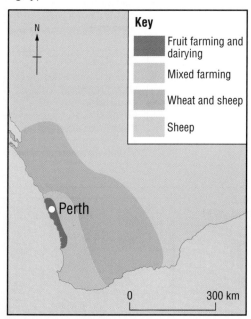

Figure 5 Rainfall distribution in south west Australia

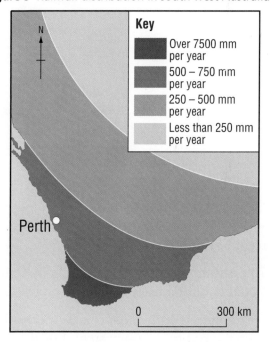

key words
intensive
arable
fodder
factor
human factors
physical factors

Old industry

main idea

Industries grew up initially near the raw materials they needed.

The iron and steel industry

This industry shows us how important it has been in the past to be near raw materials.

Figure 1 shows the changes in the location of the iron and steel industry.

1 Use the information on this page to explain the changes of locations in Figure 1.

2 Look at Figure 2. At what stage do you think the following iron or steel-making sites developed?
   a) Sheffield;
   b) Forest of Dean;
   c) Llanwern;
   d) Teesside.

Figure 1
Changes in the location of the iron and steel industry

Forest and iron ore eg Forest of Dean

Coalfield site with local iron ore and limestone. Small foundries eg Merthyr Tydfil

Coastal site Iron ore imported by ship. Coal from valley coalfields. Large flat site for integrated steelworks eg Margam

Iron ore imports

The iron-making industry has been in existence for over 2000 years. In the early days charcoal was used to smelt the iron.

In 1709 Abraham Darby found that coke made from coal could be used instead of charcoal.

In the late nineteenth century new methods were discovered to produce steel. Local deposits of iron and coal were running out in some areas and the cost of bringing imported materials from the coast was high.

After 1945, larger **integrated** works were designed. This means that all the processes of making steel are carried out at the same place. These works needed to be located in very large areas close to the deep water docks where raw materials could be imported.

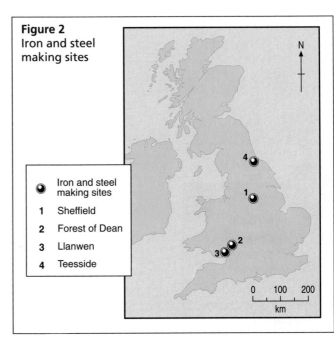

Figure 2
Iron and steel making sites

	Iron and steel making sites
1	Sheffield
2	Forest of Dean
3	Llanwen
4	Teesside

N

0 100 200
km

The woollen industry

Before you read this section ask your teacher for a copy of Worksheet 2/4.8 and follow the instructions on it.

In the seventeenth century, there were a number of parts of Britain producing woollen cloth. Two of the most important were the West Country and East Anglia.

> **3** Mark these two areas on the worksheet with the help of an atlas.

Yorkshire was also a wool-producing area. There were sheep on the Pennine Hills, and the streams running over the millstone grit produced soft water for washing the wool. The wool was produced in the farmhouses on the upper slopes of the river valleys.

> **4** Mark Yorkshire on your map, again using an atlas.

In the eighteenth century, Yorkshire began to take over as the most important wool producer in Britain. The industry also moved from the hillsides to the valleys and from cottages to factories.

> **5** Figure 3 shows this change. Use it to write a few sentences to explain the changes. Two key ideas are **water power** and **steam power**.
>
> **6** Why do you think East Anglia was the first major area to decline?
>
> **7** Why did Yorkshire become more important than the West Country?

Today although still important, the industry has declined from its position at the beginning of the twentieth century. It has had to compete with cheaper goods from foreign countries and many of the factories and machinery were old and out-dated.

Figure 3
Changes in the woollen industry

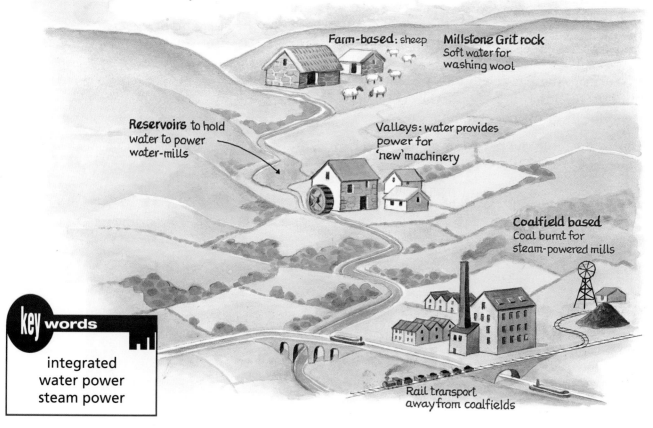

Farm-based: sheep Millstone Grit rock
Soft water for washing wool

Reservoirs to hold water to power water-mills

Valleys: water provides power for 'new' machinery

Coalfield based
Coal burnt for steam-powered mills

Rail transport away from coalfields

key words

integrated
water power
steam power

New industry

Figure 1
a) Computer
b) Washing machine
c) Calculator

main idea

Hi-tech industries tend to locate in three main areas.

High technology (hi-tech) industries rely on the **microchip**. This is a very small piece of silicon which holds a great amount of information to make appliances do their job.

Figure 1 shows some products which use microchips. Can you think of some more? You will need a copy of the table from worksheet 2/4.8.

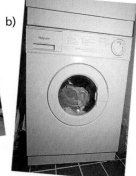

1 a) Write down the name of the appliance.
b) Write down what it does.
c) What did people do before this appliance was invented?

As a class, you have probably come up with lots of ideas. It should be clear that the microchip and the micro-electronics industry are important to our lives.

Thirty years ago these hi-tech industries did not exist and so when they first set up, they could choose to locate at the most suitable sites.

Go back to the table you have completed.

2 a) Are these appliances very large?
b) Are the electronic parts heavy?
c) Do they take up much space?

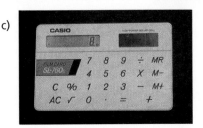

Figure 4
Pleasant shopping area

Figure 2
High quality smart houses

key words

high technology
(hi-tech)
microchip
research

Figure 3
Golf course

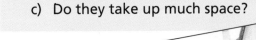

Figure 5
Motorways

The answer to all of these is no. Because of this the industry does not need to locate near to the raw materials. However, it does need to be close to good communications such as roads, railways and airports.

Most of the workers in the industry are highly-skilled technicians, scientists and professional people.

Hi-tech industries are thinking of new ideas all the time. You have only to look at computers to see how quickly new models out-date the old ones.

To keep ahead of competitors, firms need to keep up to date with new **research**. For this reason they often have links with university research departments. Universities are also useful as a source of highly-trained new workers.

Although hi-tech industry has spread throughout the UK, three areas are especially important:

- Silicon Glen (Central Scotland);
- Silicon Fen (Cambridge);
- the M4 Corridor.

Figure 6 Major locations of hi-tech industries

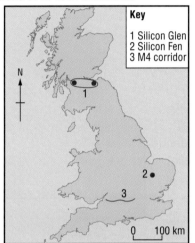

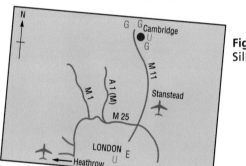

Figure 7
Silicon Fen

4 Look at Figures 6, 7, 8 and 9. Write a paragraph explaining the advantages of each site.

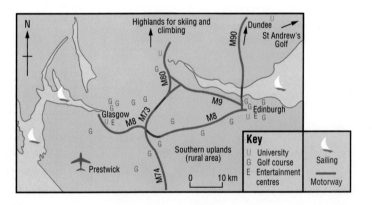

Figure 8
Silicon Glen

3 Look at Figures 2, 3, 4 and 5. You are responsible for building a new hi-tech factory and you have to attract well-qualified workers. You have to produce a brochure to send to possible new recruits.
   a) Complete a copy of table (ii) from the worksheet.
   b) For each picture say whether or not you would use it in your brochure and explain the reason why.

Figure 9 M4 Corridor

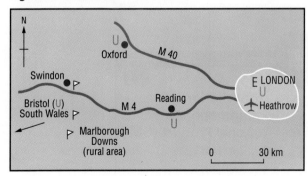

Transnationals

Companies can control businesses in many other countries.

Transnational companies (TNCs) are international businesses. They have factories or offices throughout the world. Their head office is almost always in an economically developed country. They can also be called **multinationals**. One example is Nestlé (Figure 1).

Transnationals are important.
- They employ huge numbers of people. Nestlé employs over 200 000.
- They are wealthier than many countries. Royal Dutch/Shell has sales of $104 billion, more than the **Gross National Product** (GNP) of Norway.
- They control 70 per cent of the world's trade. A lot of this trade is between different parts of the same company.

Figure 1
Nestlé's operations: a Swiss company operating in 126 countries around the world. Its raw materials come from many different countries. It makes products in many different countries. It sells products all over the world

key words

transnational
multinational
Gross National Product (GNP)
export
import

Figure 2
The richest countries (total GNP)

Country	GNP ($bn)
USA	5446
Japan	3141
USSR	1466
Germany	1486
France	1100
Italy	971
UK	924
Canada	543
Spain	429
China	416

Figure 3
The richest companies

Company	Sales ($ billion)	Country
General Motors	125	USA
Royal Dutch/Shell	107	UK/Neth
Exxon	106	USA
Ford	98	USA
IBM	69	USA
Toyota	65	Japan
IRI	61	Italy
BP	60	UK
Mobil	59	USA
General Electric	58	USA

1 Use Figures 2 and 3 and a map of the world.
   a) Mark with a star the countries where the top ten transnationals are based.
   b) Colour in the top ten countries.
2 Write a sentence about the pattern of countries on your map. Use the terms 'economically developed countries' and 'economically developing countries'.
3 Write a sentence about the distribution of the biggest transnationals. Use the same terms as you did in Question 2.

The maquiladora industry of Mexico

'Maquiladora' are factories which grew up in Mexico along the border with the USA (see Figure 4). They were allowed to **import** raw materials and **export** finished products without paying duty. Customs duty is a fee which usually has to be paid on imported or exported goods.

waste. Only 300 have official licences. What are the effects in Mexico?

- Environmental pollution with terrible effects on health, particularly affecting children.
- Huge growth of the small towns with poor housing areas. They lack the most basic services like clean water.

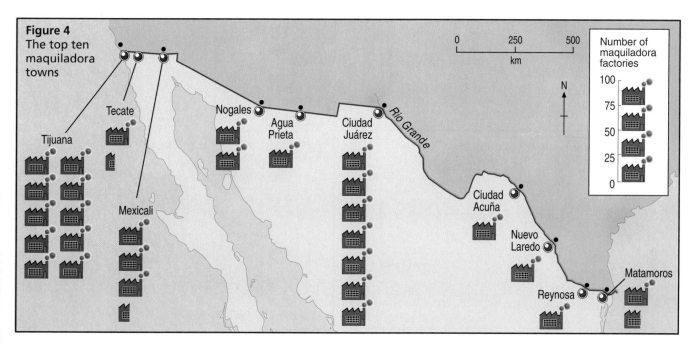

Figure 4
The top ten maquiladora towns

These factories are either American-owned or owned by transnationals with factories in the USA. The most important industries are the motor, electronic and textile. Between 1982 and 1992 the number of workers in the factories grew from 120 000 to 500 000.

4 a) Why were the factories located on the border and not throughout Mexico?
b) Most of the border towns have American 'twins' across the border. Use an atlas and find their names.

There are two main reasons why all these companies built factories in Mexico.

- Low wages. Many workers earn as little as $30 a week. In the USA the same companies pay ten times more.
- Weak environmental laws. Many companies ignore regulations that exist. Out of more than 2000 foreign factories, half produce hazardous

5 Copy and complete the flow diagram in Figure 5. Use information from the section above to help you.

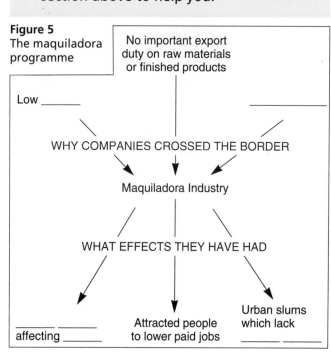

Figure 5
The maquiladora programme

No important export duty on raw materials or finished products

Low _____

_____ _____

WHY COMPANIES CROSSED THE BORDER

Maquiladora Industry

WHAT EFFECTS THEY HAVE HAD

_____ _____
affecting _____

Attracted people to lower paid jobs

Urban slums which lack _____ _____

The 'Four Tigers'

Other countries in South East Asia are also **industrialising** rapidly. Malaysia and Thailand are now growing fast, as is Indonesia.

Figure 1
The 'Four Tigers' and other rapidly industrialising countries

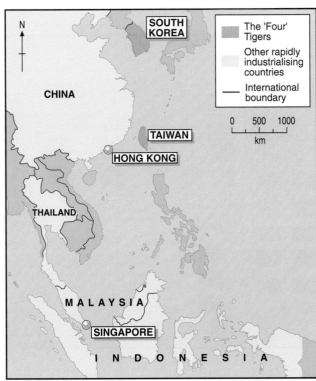

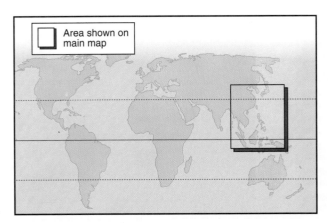

Figure 2
Changes in the countries of South East Asia

Country	GNP per person ($)		Export growth (%)		Infant mortality (per 1000 births)		Women in secondary education (%)	
Years	1973	1994	1970–80	1982–92	1970	1991	1970	1991
Singapore	1580	18 025	9.9	4.2	14	7	45	75
Hong Kong	1560	18 500	9.7	5.0	15	7	—	—
South Korea	460	7250	23.5	11.9	40	17	32	88
Taiwan	—	11 236	15.6	11.0	—	—	—	—
Thailand	240	2085	10.3	14.7	55	27	15	32
Malaysia	550	3230	4.8	11.3	37	16	28	59

The 'Four Tigers' is the name given to Hong Kong, South Korea, Taiwan and Singapore (see Figure 1). The industries of these countries have grown in a very short time. Well-known companies include Samsung from Taiwan and Hyundai from South Korea.

key word

industrialising

1 Statistics are useful but pictures are often easier to understand.

Divide into small groups in your class and produce a display based on Figure 1. Decide for yourselves how to do it. But you must cover the following points.
a) The displays must show and describe all six countries. A map of South East Asia should be used.
b) Present each country in the same way.
c) Add some written notes and graphs. Include a list of points about the changes occurring in each country and describe how the four sets of figures in Figure 2 are linked.

The giant of the future is China. The south of China is one of the fastest-growing industrial regions in the world.

Figure 2 shows some changes that have taken place in these countries of South East Asia.

Your displays show lots of improvements. But there are also difficulties and problems in these countries.

One problem is tied to the way in which industry developed in the first place.

An example can show what happens. A textile factory moved from Japan to South Korea to a city outside Seoul. This was because wages were a lot lower in South Korea.

However, the factory used methods which caused illness and death amongst the workers. The factory also caused a lot of air pollution in the area. After a lot of protests the factory was closed.

Now the factory is being moved to China. Wages are very low there and there are no controls on health risks.

This sort of thing happened in all the 'Four Tigers'. The early industries caused pollution and depended on cheap labour. Now they are being moved by their owners to other countries. Many are owned by transnationals.

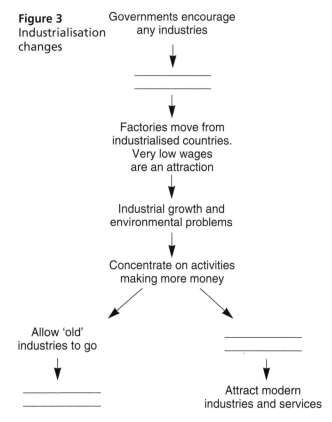

Figure 3
Industrialisation changes

Figure 4
Labels for Question 2

- 'Dirty' factories move to another cheaper country.
- It does not matter about the environment.
- Develop education and training to attract more valuable jobs

2 Figures 3 and 4 show these ideas in a different way. Make a large copy of Figure 3 and use the labels from Figure 4 to complete it.

In the 'Four Tigers' the important work has changed. Figure 5 shows the changes.

Figure 5
How the 'Tigers' are changing

Country	Change to	Examples
Taiwan	High technology industry	Electronics
Singapore	High technology industry and services	Banking
Hong Kong	Services	Banking
Korea	Heavy industries	Steel

RESOURCES AND THE ENVIRONMENT
Types of resources

main idea

What are resources and how are they classified?

In order to live, we **need** certain things.

1 Make a list of the things you need to live.

You probably included in your list things to eat, drink and to keep you warm.

There are also things that we *want* so that our lives are better. If you started to make a complete list of these, you could still be writing at the end of the lesson!

Here is something to help you keep the list short.

2 Imagine that you were marooned on a small island. What things would you miss?
a) Make a list of these things. Try to keep your list to the ten most important things you can think of.

Figure 1
a) Coal mine b) Gas holder
c) Farmland d) Forest
e) Reservoir f) Quarry

Figure 2
Rainforest hardwood

Figure 3
British softwood

Our needs and wants are met by using materials found on and in the earth. These are called **resources**.

In your list of wants, you might have included cars, radios and TVs. These themselves are not resources but resources are needed to make and run them.

> **3** Look at Figure 1. Make a list of the resources that you can see in the photographs.
>
> Alongside the resource put an **N** if you think we need it or a **W** if you think we only want it.

Perhaps we have become so used to all of these resources that we feel that we need them all!

Some resources can be used more than once. Farmers can use their fields to grow crops or graze animals year after year.

We call these resources **renewable**.

Some resources, once they are used, are gone for good. If stone is removed from a quarry and used to help build a road, then it cannot be used again.

Gas, oil and coal are other examples of resources that can only be used once. We shall look at these again in the next unit.

Resources that can only be used once are called **non-renewable**.

Figures 2 and 3 show two different types of forest. Both are renewable resources but of course trees take a long time to grow! Also the cutting down of trees in the rainforest have other effects which you can see in Chapter 5, Unit 7.

One of the uses of softwoods is to make paper. But old, used paper can be reused to make new paper. This is called **recycling**.

> **4** Look at Figure 4.
> a) What are the goods that are being recycled?
> b) What resources are being recycled?

Figure 4
Recycling village

key words

need
resources
renewable
non-renewable
recycling

Chapter 5 unit 2

Electricity

main idea

There are different ways of producing electricity.

Energy is needed to make things work. If you work hard or exercise, like going for a run, then you get hot and use up energy. Afterwards you need to eat and drink to help replace the energy you have used.

Like you, machines also need energy to make them work.

Electricity is one of the most important sources of energy. It is produced by using many of the earth's resources.

Most of our electricity is made by boiling water to produce steam which drives a power station generator.

Figure 1 shows the ways in which resources are used to heat the water.

1 Name each resource and say whether it is non-renewable or renewable.

Figure 2
Life expectancy of fossil fuels

Fossil fuel	Last year of use
Oil	2035
Gas	2050
Coal	2050

Apart from nuclear power, the other resources you named in Question 1 are **fossil fuels**. You will probably remember that coal is formed from the remains of trees and plants. Oil and natural gas were formed from the remains of dead sea creatures. These fossil fuels take millions of years to form but we are using them up quickly.

Figure 1
a) Gas holder b) Coal mine c) Oil well d) Nuclear power station

a)

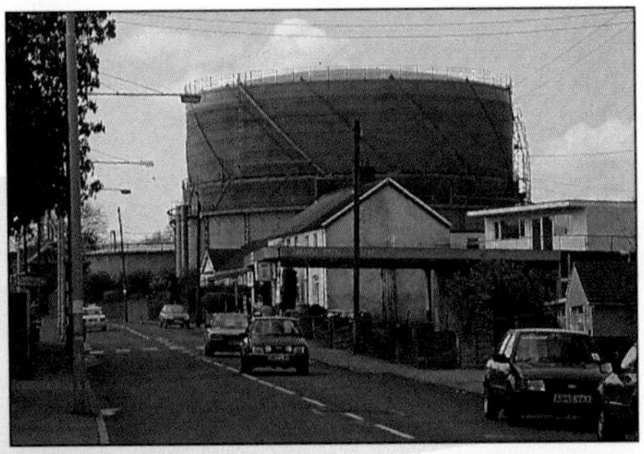

b)

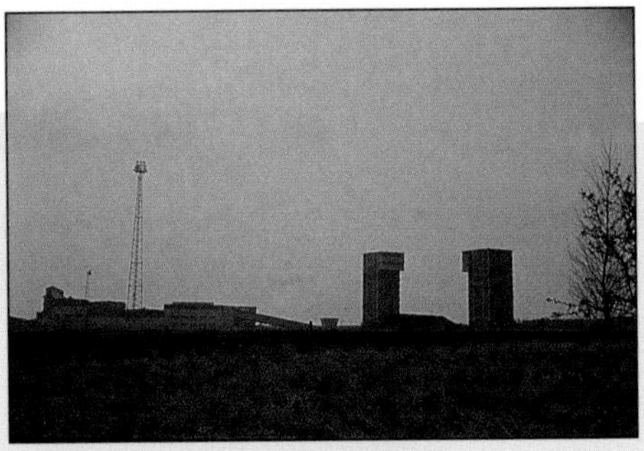

c)

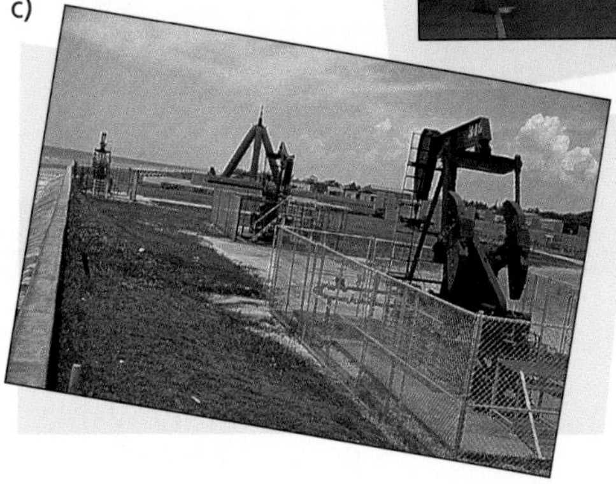

d)

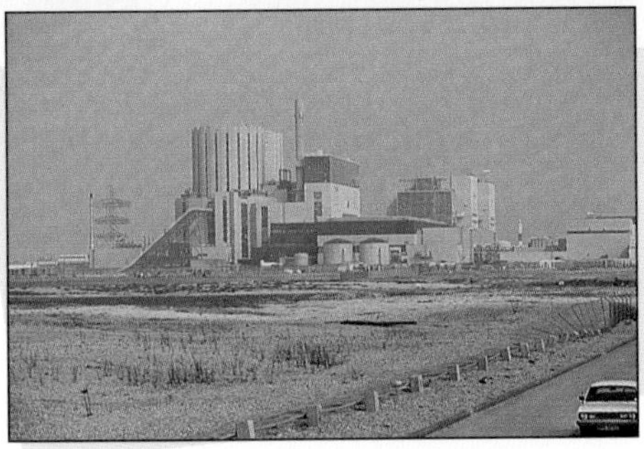

Figure 2 shows how long fossil fuels will last if we continue to use them at the present rate.

> **2** Draw a bar graph to show how many more years we have left of each of the fossil fuels. Label it 'How long our fossil fuels will last.'

We could extend the life of these fuels if we cut down on our use of energy. One way to do this would be to find other ways to produce electricity.

Nuclear power uses a non-renewable resource (uranium). We have only been mining uranium for about 60 years but we know that we have at least 1000 years supply of it (add this information to your bar chart).

Not everybody is happy about producing nuclear power (see Directions Book 1, Chapter 2, Unit 9).

If we want to go on producing electricity for ever, we need to use renewable resources – those that will never run out.

Water, wind and the sun are all renewable sources. They can all be used to produce electricity – some have been used more successfully than others.

Hydro-electric power (HEP) is produced by using fast-flowing water to turn a generator (see Figure 3).

Figure 4
Windmill

Figure 5
Wind-powered phone

b)

a)

Figure 3
Hydro-electric power station

In the past windmills were used to turn machines (Figure 4). Now they are being used to produce electricity (Figure 5). One problem is that nearly 2000 wind turbines would be needed to produce as much electricity as one nuclear power station.

Figure 6
Solar power

> **3** Can you think of another problem with wind turbines? (CLUE: When are sailing boats unable to sail?)
>
> **4** Figure 6 shows a device for producing electricity from the sun (**solar power**). Can you think of any problems that this may cause in the UK?

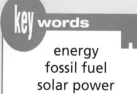

key words

energy
fossil fuel
solar power

79

Development of resources

The development of resources depends on a variety of factors.

Over time, farmers have worked to drain and clear their land. Why did the farmer decide to leave some of the land in the picture uncleared (Figure 1)? There will have been a number of factors to consider when deciding whether to improve some of the land or not.

Figure 1
Farming land

Figure 2
Profitable or not?

Figure 3
Where did Britain's oil come from?

0   1500   3000
km

N

IRAN

LIBYA

MIDDLE
EAST

VENEZUELA

NIGERIA

Usually the most important question is *'Will it make a profit?'* There isn't much point in spending time and money on improving the land if it will not make money for the farmer.

How much can I sell it for?

Where can I sell it?

How much will it cost to produce?

Is there a demand for the product?

key words

profit
development

You can see some of the questions that farmers need to answer before they know whether or not a **profit** can be made in Figure 2.

The **development** of other resources throughout the world, follow similar patterns.

The North Sea is now an important oil field. The problems of developing the field have included:
- drilling at sea;
- gale force winds;
- rigs icing up in winter;
- problems of getting oil ashore;
- problems of getting workers to and from the rigs.

> **1** Use the information from Figures 3, 4 and 5 to explain why it was worth developing the North Sea oil field.

Figure 4
The cost of oil, 1973–1981

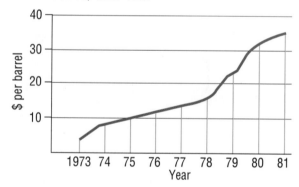

Sweden has a large number of conifer forests. The wood is used in the paper-making industry. There are three stages in making paper.
1 Cutting down trees.
2 Turning the wood into pulp.
3 Turning the pulp into paper.

The wood starts off in a very bulky form but as it goes through the processes it gets less bulky.

> **2 a)** Which do you think is easier to transport: i) felled timber; or ii) paper?
>
> **b)** Which would you pay more for: i) wood pulp; or ii) paper?

Figure 5
International crisis

Date	Event	Where
1973	War between Israel and Egypt. Oil-producing countries threaten to cut off oil supplies to countries supporting Israel.	Middle East
1978	Ruler of Iran overthrown Oil supplies interrupted.	Middle East
1980	War between Iran and Iraq.	Middle East
1990	Iraq invaded Kuwait. United Nations banned trade with Iraq.	Middle East

In both cases you have probably answered paper.

When it is cut, timber may well be some distance from roads or tracks. It has to be transported from the forest to the pulp mills where it is chewed up in machinery which uses a great deal of electricity.

> **3** Use Figure 6 to help you explain why Sweden is a good country for using timber resources to produce paper.

Figure 6
Sweden's timber industry

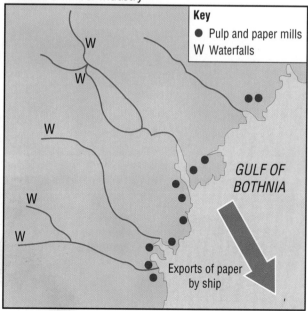

Resources and the environment

> The environment can be harmed or improved by using resources.

We have seen how important resources are to our lives but what are the effects of using them? In the past industrial towns were often dirty and unpleasant areas. Now planners try to ensure that the development of resources will benefit the local area.

Figure 1 is a picture of a gravel pit. The gravel is being taken from the ground to help to build roads and buildings.

Figure 1
Gravel pit

Figure 2
Holme Pierrepont
water sports centre

Figure 3
Holme Pierrepont
water sports centre

key words

exhausted
Aral Sea
irrigate

When all of the gravel is used up the site is known as **exhausted**. What happens to the sites when this happens? A development alongside the River Trent at Nottingham shows how the area can be put to good use for the enjoyment of a variety of people. At one time the area had been a series of pits from where sand and gravel was taken.

You will need a copy of Worksheet 2/5.4 to see how the site has been put to good use.

The **Aral Sea** is an example of an area which has not been well managed. Figure 4 shows its position in Kazakhstan in Central Asia.

Figure 4 The Aral Sea

1 What are the names of the two main rivers flowing into the Aral Sea?

Rice and cotton are grown in the Aral Sea region on land reclaimed from the desert. Water is fed onto the land by diverting the two main rivers for **irrigation**. Before they were diverted these rivers poured over 50 km^3 of water into the sea each year. By 1990 the flow was only about 30 per cent of that (i.e. about 18 km^3). In 1960, Aralsk was a thriving fishing town on the edge of the Aral Sea. Its markets contained the produce from the surrounding area, e.g. fish, fruit and vegetables. Now it has little produce to sell. The sea is 60 km away, there are boats left on the old sea bed and the surrounding area is a desert.

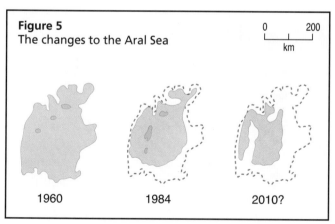

Figure 5
The changes to the Aral Sea

0   200
km

1960   1984   2010?

2 Look at Figure 5. Use this and the information above to explain why the Aral Sea is getting smaller.

The shrinking sea has had an effect on the climate up to 100 km away from the sea (Figure 6).

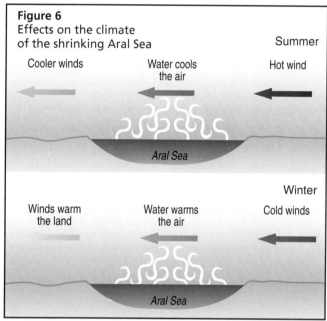

Figure 6
Effects on the climate of the shrinking Aral Sea

Summer

Cooler winds   Water cools the air   Hot wind

Aral Sea

Winter

Winds warm the land   Water warms the air   Cold winds

Aral Sea

3 Use the information from Figure 6 to complete this statement by choosing the correct words.

'Warm air crossing the sea in **winter/ summer** was cooled. In winter the air crossing the sea was **cooled/warmed** and warmed the surrounding land. Now that the sea is smaller it is unable to have such an effect on the land. Summers are now **hotter/colder** and the winters are longer and **warmer/colder**.'

Even the scheme to irrigate the land for rice and cotton has not worked well. Over 40 per cent of the water is lost to the sand before it reaches the crops.

Before the irrigation scheme, the region was able to produce fruit and vegetables and supplied large areas of the country with fish. Unless something is done now the region around the Aral Sea will soon become a desert.

Here you have seen just two examples of the way in which the use of resources affects the environment. It is important that we develop resources in a way that cares for the environment in the long term.

Resources and the local area

Are open-cast mining methods the future of British coal mining?

For the last 200 years or more, coal has been taken from the ground by tunnelling into the earth. **Open-cast** mining uses heavy machinery to take away the top layers of soil and rock to reach the coal (see Figure 1).

Figure 2 shows where the shallow deposits of coal are found in Britain.

Figure 1
Open-cast mining machinery

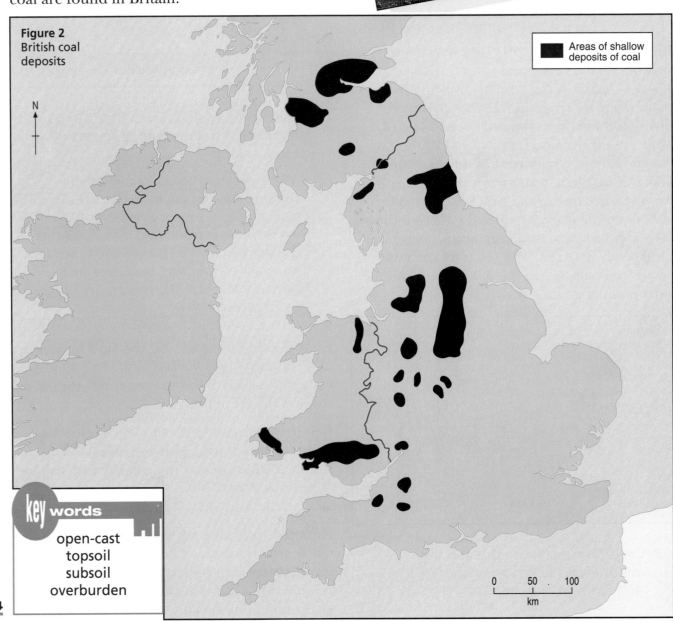

Figure 2
British coal deposits

N

Areas of shallow deposits of coal

0   50   100
km

key words

open-cast
topsoil
subsoil
overburden

There are a number of advantages to using open-cast coal production.

- Low production costs help it to compete with imported coal.
- Coal is of good quality. Only clean coal is mined rather than a mixture of rock and coal as in deep mines.
- Deep mines need at least a 1 m thick band of coal in order to be worth mining. Open-cast mines can take out seams only 10 cm thick (see Figure 3).

Figure 3
Narrow seam

- Open-cast sites can be returned quickly to their use before mining or the site can be used for recreational purposes.

When an open-cast site is first developed, the **topsoil** is removed and stored as embankments around the edge of the site.

> **1** What advantage will these embankments have for local residents?

Subsoil is also stored. These soils will be replaced when the site is restored after mining.

Once the soils have been removed, the **overburden** (the rocks above the coal), is removed (Figure 4). This is stored and used to refill the site when the coal has been removed.

Figure 4
Coal overburden

Figure 5
Bleak House
open-cast site in
Staffordshire

As coal is removed from each section, the area is backfilled with the overburden. Finally when coal has been removed from the whole site, the subsoil and topsoil are replaced.

Bleak House open-cast site (Figure 5) is in Staffordshire.

Permission to mine the coal at Bleak House was given provided that the mining company agreed to:

- protect an important pool of water by building two storage reservoirs;
- store heathland and create a nursery for heathland plants.

Figure 6
Former
open-cast
mining sites

When the mining is complete at Bleak House, the site will be returned to natural heathland with woods and a number of water pools.

Coal is removed from the mine by a private road leading to a coal disposal plant at the railway in Cannock.

Not all open-cast sites are restored to their former uses.

Look at the uses that one former site has been put to in Figure 6.

> **2** Can you think of how you would like to see open-cast sites used?

5 Pollution

Pollution affects wide areas.

Pollution occurs when any substance that causes damage is released into the environment. It can affect:

- air;
- water; and
- land.

Polluted air, water and land can, in turn, affect people, animals and plants.

Pollution in Russia

Nikel is a Russian town on the Kola peninsula in the Murmansk region (see Figure 1). It is 30 km from the border with Norway.

Figure 1
The location of Nikel in Russia

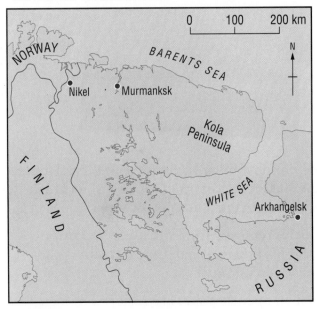

Nikel is one of the world's biggest producers of nickel. The effects of this industry on the local environment have been enormous.

- 500 000 tonnes of sulphur dioxide are pumped into the air every year. You can smell the sulphur up to 30 km away. It has destroyed 700 km² of forest.

- Heavy metals like copper and cobalt have killed all the fish in the rivers and lakes.
- Reindeer herders in Norway have had their way of life destroyed. The lichen their herds graze on has been killed by **acid rain**.
- Peoples' health has suffered. The average life expectancy of workers here is 47 years. 90 per cent of the population could have damaged lungs. Asthma and excema are common amongst children.
- Near the town are five spoil heaps. Each one is 2 km long and 60 m high.

1 Make a large copy of Figure 2. Label it to show how the nickel factory has affected the people and their area. Arrange your labelling according to whether the effects are the result of air, water or land pollution. Some items might go in more than one group.

There is pollution almost everywhere in Russia and other former republics of the USSR.

2 Study Figure 3 and an atlas map of the former USSR.
   a) How many areas of severe pollution are there?
   b) How large is the area that is badly affected by acid rain?
   c) Name the rivers which are polluted. Are any major rivers unpolluted?
   d) How many areas of the country have sites related to nuclear power or nuclear weapons?

There have been many accidents at nuclear power plants. **Radioactive fall-out** from the accident at the Chernobyl nuclear power station in 1986 contaminated 6.5 million ha of farmland and forest in the Ukraine. Twenty per cent of the farmland of neighbouring Belorussia was contaminated. 2.2 million people lived in the areas affected by fall-out. Many have health problems as a result.

Figure 2
Pollution sources and destinations

Figure 3
Pollution in the former USSR

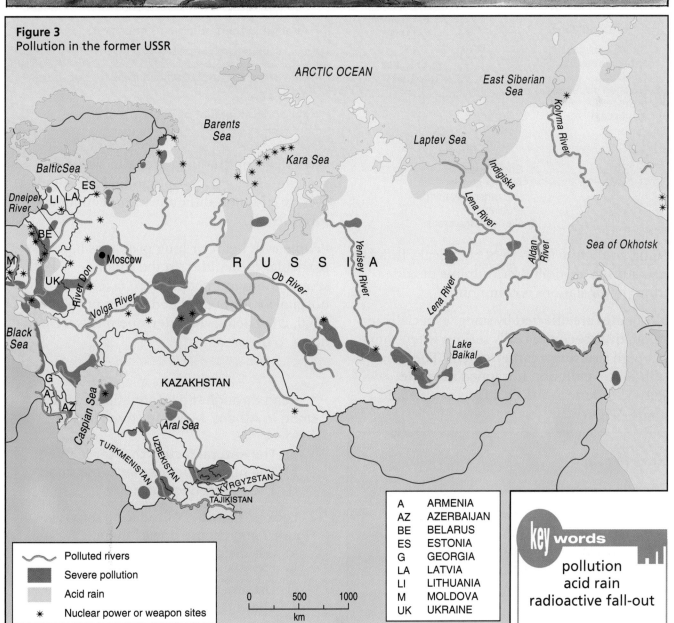

| | Polluted rivers |
| Severe pollution |
| Acid rain |
| * | Nuclear power or weapon sites |

0   500   1000
km

A	ARMENIA
AZ	AZERBAIJAN
BE	BELARUS
ES	ESTONIA
G	GEORGIA
LA	LATVIA
LI	LITHUANIA
M	MOLDOVA
UK	UKRAINE

key words

pollution
acid rain
radioactive fall-out

Causes of pollution

main idea

Pollution has many causes.

Air pollution

Locally there can be pockets of **air pollution** from single factories. Most urban areas have a more general problem of **smog** caused by motor vehicle exhaust fumes (Figure 1).

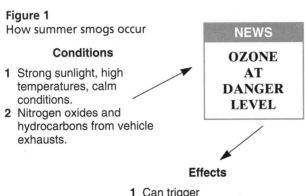

Figure 1
How summer smogs occur

Conditions

1 Strong sunlight, high temperatures, calm conditions.
2 Nitrogen oxides and hydrocarbons from vehicle exhausts.

NEWS

OZONE AT DANGER LEVEL

Effects

1 Can trigger asthma attacks and other breathing problems.
2 Can damage crops.

Smog contains a mixture of chemicals. Industry also adds to air pollution. Sulphur dioxide from power stations is common.

Most cities are affected by smog, especially in summer. It becomes really serious when there is a high pressure weather system. The air is still, so the pollution is trapped near the surface, where it directly affects people and plants (Figure 2).

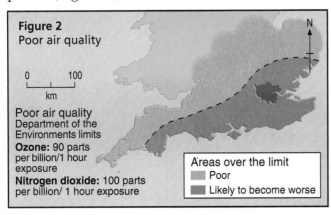

Figure 2
Poor air quality

0   100
km

Poor air quality
Department of the Environments limits
Ozone: 90 parts per billion/1 hour exposure
Nitrogen dioxide: 100 parts per billion/ 1 hour exposure

Areas over the limit
Poor
Likely to become worse

Athens

Athens has very hot summers, terrible traffic congestion and over half of Greece's industry. The result is a bad smog problem (Figure 3).

Figure 3
Athens – the future

What has been tried?

• Using more air conditioners and fans.
• Banning cars and taxis from the city centre on alternate days.
• Abolishing the traditional 3 hour siesta.

What has been suggested?

• Industrial relocation (moving industry out of the Athens area).
• Major development of public transport.

The effects of the smog are unpleasant and sometimes deadly. Symptoms include stinging eyes, tired limbs, difficulty with sleeping and sore throats.

People with heart or lung problems have particular difficulties. In the summer of 1994 several thousand people were taken into hospital with smog-related health problems. In 1990, 2000 deaths of elderly people were put down to the smog.

1 Read through the information about smog in Athens. Make out three lists as follows.
   a) The natural factors that cause smog.
   b) The human factors that cause smog.
   c) The effects of smog.

2 Look at the ways of reducing smogs in Figure 3 and choose one of them.
   a) List the points in its favour.
   b) List the points against it.
   c) List any other points you can make about it.

Water pollution

Groundwater

Groundwater is the water stored in layers of rock below the land surface. It is a major source of water supplies. Harmful substances can seep down into it and build up to dangerous levels (see Figure 4).

Figure 4
Newspaper headlines

> Sewage effluent puts end to sport

> Bathers risk illness in rivers and lakes

> River chemicals 'endanger human health'

> Chemicals kill all life in 4-mile stretch of river

> Fears over the toxic cocktail

> Nitrate worst in East Anglia water

Some pollutants in groundwater come from agriculture. **Nitrates** in fertilisers dissolve easily and are not all taken up by plants. Some are washed directly into streams but some seep down into the groundwater. In Britain, East Anglia has the worst problem.

> 3 Look at Figure 5.
>   a) Why would there still be a problem if nitrate use was stopped completely?
>   b) What solutions have been used to deal with the water supply problem?
>   c) What alternative solutions might there be? Think about their good points and bad points as well as any other related issues.

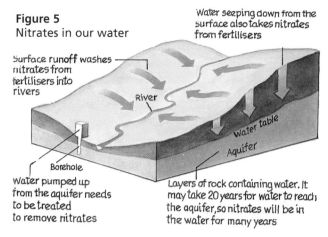

Figure 5
Nitrates in our water

Water seeping down from the surface also takes nitrates from fertilisers

Surface runoff washes nitrates from fertilisers into rivers

River

Water table

Aquifer

Borehole

Water pumped up from the aquifer needs to be treated to remove nitrates

Layers of rock containing water. It may take 20 years for water to reach the aquifer, so nitrates will be in the water for many years

Rivers and lakes

Harmful substances can enter a river directly as a one-off accident, but the effects are still devastating. Pollution may also stem from legal dumping, building up over many years.

River **estuaries** are often a big problem. All the tributaries of the main river send their pollution to the same place.

> 4 Look at the map of the Humber and its tributaries in Figure 6 and an atlas map of the same area.
>   a) Industry and urban areas produce most river pollution. Which rivers do you think could be polluted? Mark them on your own copy of the map.
>   b) What are the possible sources of pollution shown on Figure 6?

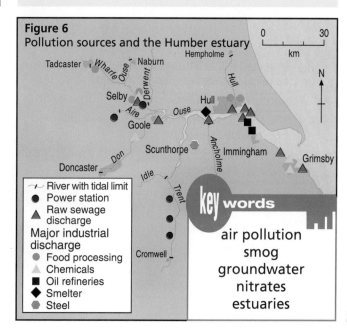

Figure 6
Pollution sources and the Humber estuary

0   30
km

Tadcaster   Wharfe   Ouse   Naburn   Hempholme   Hull

Selby   Derwent   Hull   N

Aire   Ouse

Goole

Don   Scunthorpe   Ancholme   Immingham   Grimsby

Doncaster   Idle

Trent

Cromwell

- River with tidal limit
- ● Power station
- ▲ Raw sewage discharge
- Major industrial discharge
- ● Food processing
- ▲ Chemicals
- ■ Oil refineries
- ◆ Smelter
- ⬢ Steel

key words

air pollution
smog
groundwater
nitrates
estuaries

A world issue

Some environmental issues affect the whole world.

Global warming

Most people have some idea about **global warming** and not everyone agrees that it is even happening. However, in 1990 a scientific report said that the **greenhouse effect** causes global warming. Levels of gases, known as greenhouse gases, particularly **carbon dioxide** and methane are rising.

Climate change is certain to occur if global warming is taking place and if greenhouse gases increase. Carbon dioxide has increased from 280 parts per million (ppm) 200 years ago to over 350 ppm in 1995. If this continues then average temperatures will rise and, as a result of melting ice caps, **sea levels** will also rise.

1 Study Figure 1. Make a copy of Figure 1b and complete it by adding labels from the list.

Figure 1
a) The greenhouse effect
b) Increased carbon dioxide emissions

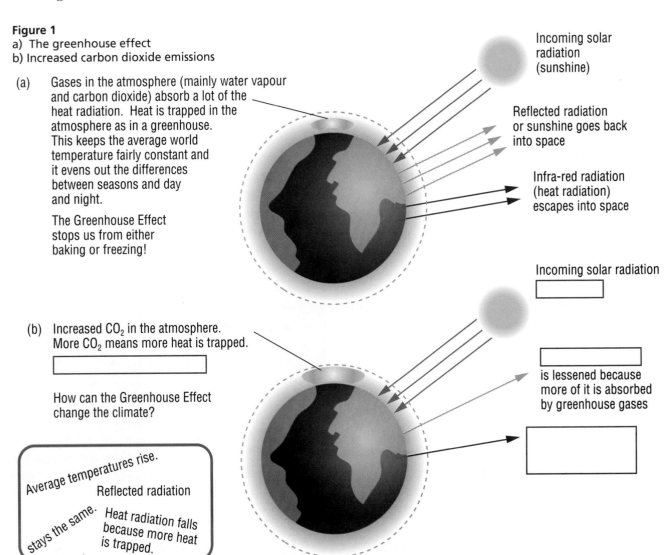

(a) Gases in the atmosphere (mainly water vapour and carbon dioxide) absorb a lot of the heat radiation. Heat is trapped in the atmosphere as in a greenhouse. This keeps the average world temperature fairly constant and it evens out the differences between seasons and day and night.

The Greenhouse Effect stops us from either baking or freezing!

(b) Increased CO₂ in the atmosphere. More CO₂ means more heat is trapped.

How can the Greenhouse Effect change the climate?

Average temperatures rise.
Reflected radiation stays the same.
Heat radiation falls because more heat is trapped.

Incoming solar radiation (sunshine)

Reflected radiation or sunshine goes back into space

Infra-red radiation (heat radiation) escapes into space

Incoming solar radiation

is lessened because more of it is absorbed by greenhouse gases

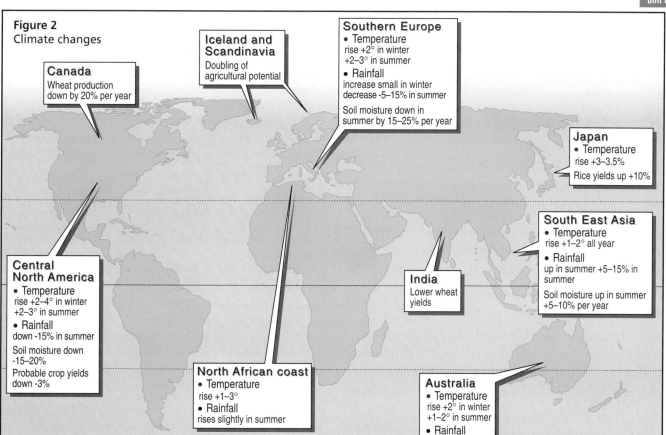

Figure 2
Climate changes

Canada
Wheat production
down by 20% per year

Iceland and Scandinavia
Doubling of
agricultural potential

Southern Europe
• Temperature
rise +2° in winter
+2–3° in summer
• Rainfall
increase small in winter
decrease -5–15% in summer

Soil moisture down in
summer by 15–25% per year

Japan
• Temperature
rise +3–3.5%
Rice yields up +10%

South East Asia
• Temperature
rise +1–2° all year
• Rainfall
up in summer +5–15% in
summer

Soil moisture up in summer
+5–10% per year

Central North America
• Temperature
rise +2–4° in winter
+2–3° in summer
• Rainfall
down -15% in summer
Soil moisture down
-15–20%
Probable crop yields
down -3%

India
Lower wheat
yields

North African coast
• Temperature
rise +1–3°
• Rainfall
rises slightly in summer

Australia
• Temperature
rise +2° in winter
+1–2° in summer
• Rainfall
up 10%

The carbon dioxide in the atmosphere comes from two huge stores.

1 The coal, oil and natural gas trapped in the earth's rocks which are now being extracted and burnt.
2 The vast forests that used to cover the earth. They have been and are still being cut down and burned. This increases the amount of CO_2 in the atmosphere.

No-one knows for sure what will happen as a result of rising temperatures. It is thought that the average temperature will rise by 1.5–4.5°C and that sea levels will rise by 0.5 m. Many important towns and cities could be affected.

The world map in Figure 2 shows the possible effects of the changes that could happen to climates around the world.

There are many factors involved, so predicting the effect of global warming on climate zones is extremely difficult. One problem could be the effect of climate change on the major food-producing areas.

2 You will need an atlas. Find the most useful maps telling you about the locations of major cities and food-producing areas.
   a) Name some of the major cities which could be affected by rising sea levels.
   b) Name major food-producing areas which could be affected by climate change.

key words

global warming
greenhouse effect
carbon dioxide
climatic change
sea level

Dry lands

Dry lands have fragile environments.

Not long ago people thought that the deserts were spreading. The Sahara Desert, for example, seemed to be growing.

It was really more complicated than this. Areas that were over-used, perhaps by over-grazing, seemed to turn into desert. However, with a few years of good rainfall and soil care, many places improved.

Desertification was the word used to describe land thought to be turning to desert. The areas at **risk** are called **marginal lands**. They are areas where rainfall is light and varies a lot from year to year.

Land degradation happens after land appears to become desert. Vegetation changes or even disappears. Soil is eroded. Farming and grazing then become impossible.

Figure 1
Processes of land degradation

(a) Overgrazing

(i) Overgrazing removes much of the vegetation
Poor vegetaion cover

(ii) Without a vegetation cover rainwater runs off down slope
Rain water runs off

(iii) Soil stripped away and gullies cut. Wind blows away fine soil material
Soil stripped
Gullying

(b) Arable farming

(i) Land ploughed and left without vegetation to hold it together
Clear, ploughed land

(ii) Before crops grow, rain runoff removes soil and cuts gullies
Runoff, soil erosion

(iii) Soils removed from higher land. Lower land covered by sand and pebbles
Erosion
Sediment deposited

(c) Irrigation

(i) Land levelled for irrigation. High temperatures, high rate of evaporation

(ii) Water drawn up by evaporation at surface
Soil water moves up

(iii) Salts deposited at the surface as a product of evaporation, leaving soil useless for cultivation
Salts deposited

There are human and environmental reasons for this. One is an increase in the number of people and so a heavier use of the land results. Another is a change of land use in some way.

Figure 2
Gullying

Figure 3
Grazing steep lightly vegetated slopes

1 Study Figure 1 carefully. Explain why the land in Figure 3 is at risk.

2 Look at Figure 1b. Explain how the gully in Figure 2 could have been formed.

3 Look at Figure 1c and make your own copy of Figure 4. Use Figure 1c to complete the labelling on Figure 4.

key words

desertification
risk
marginal lands
land degradation
technology
arid

Figure 4
Salt instead of crops

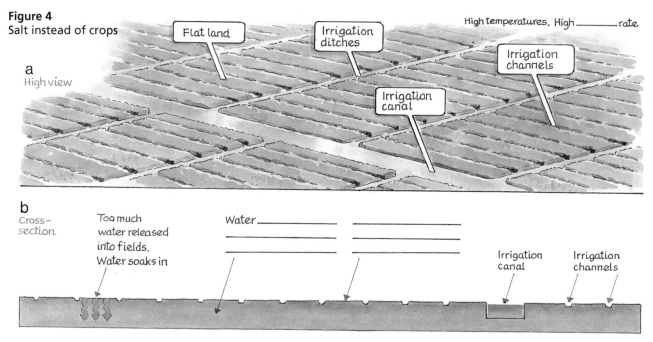

a
High view

Flat land

Irrigation ditches

High temperatures. High _____ rate

Irrigation channels

Irrigation canal

b
Cross-section

Too much water released into fields. Water soaks in

Water _____

Irrigation canal

Irrigation channels

4 Study the plan in Figure 5. Make lists of the following:
   a) where the water comes from;
   b) how water use is conserved;
   c) how damage from outside is limited;
   d) how soil is protected from erosion.

The modern irrigation scheme (see Figure 4) shows how **technology** can cause problems. But farming can be very productive in dry areas if the right methods are used.

Figure 5 is a plan for a farm development in an **arid** or semi-arid area. It avoids damaging the environment. It also avoids being damaged.

Figure 5
A modern desert farm

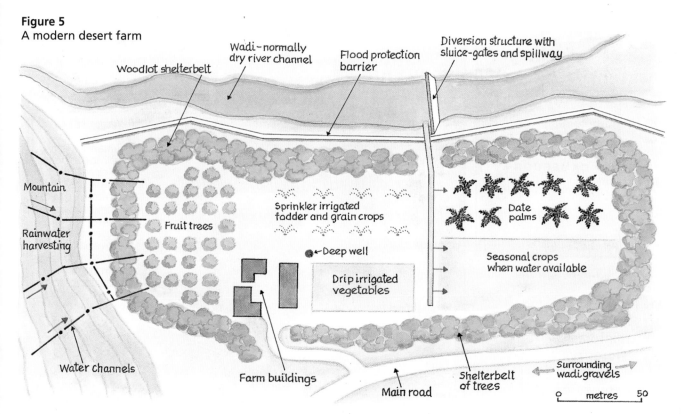

Woodlot shelterbelt

Wadi – normally dry river channel

Flood protection barrier

Diversion structure with sluice-gates and spillway

Mountain

Rainwater harvesting

Fruit trees

Sprinkler irrigated fodder and grain crops

Deep well

Drip irrigated vegetables

Date palms

Seasonal crops when water available

Water channels

Farm buildings

Main road

Shelterbelt of trees

Surrounding wadi gravels

0 metres 50

Rainforests

main idea

Tropical rainforests could disappear in the next 20 years.

The **rainforests** of the tropical world are being cut down at a very fast rate. The actual removal occurs for several reasons:

- clearing by peasant farmers for farmland;
- clearing by cutting and burning to give grazing for cattle, usually by large companies;
- felling by timber companies mainly for building materials;
- felling for firewood.

The effects of removing rainforests are listed in Figure 1.

Figure 1
Effects of rainforest removal

- Soil erosion where the forest has been removed.
- Flooding in areas downstream.
- Silting up of rivers by eroded soil.
- Loss of plant and animal species.
- Loss of human habitat for local peoples.
- Climate change in the area cleared and throughout the region.
- Global warming as a result of increased carbon dioxide in the atmosphere.

Figure 2
Korup Rainforest Park, Cameroon

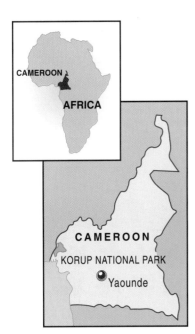

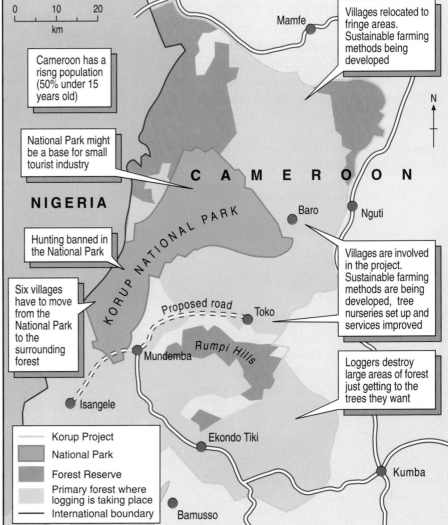

key words

rainforests
forestry
sustainable
conservation

Possible solutions

Forest parks

Most of West Africa's primary forest has disappeared. One way of protecting what is left is to set up Rainforest Parks. Korup in Cameroon is one example (Figure 2).

> **1** Look at Figure 2. Think about the issues involved.
> a) What are the advantages of setting up Rainforest Parks?
> b) What problems will have to be dealt with?
> c) What opportunities will they present?

Sustainable forestry

Around the world there are many small **forestry** projects. They may hold the key to the future because they make forestry **sustainable** (see Figure 3). The projects keep forestry in the hands of local people.

Figure 3
Clear logging and sustainable logging

Clear logging	Sustainable logging
Removes *all* trees	Takes a *few* mature trees
⇓	⇓
Destroys young trees, wasting future resources	Allows young trees to grow to maturity
⇓	⇓
Causes widespread damage to the environment: soil erosion, flooding	Allows other activities to carry on, e.g. hunting, fishing, farming, because the environment is unharmed
⇓	⇓
Provides work for a short time before the area is cleared of timber	Provides long-term income for local community

One example is a community project in Papua New Guinea in which a British company, B&Q, are involved. The local people have been given help to set up a small-scale logging company. B&Q have put money into the project and they sell products using the timber (see Figure 4).

The project is run by the local people who manage their logging carefully. No long-term damage is done and **conservation** is central to their methods. It means they can extract timber year after year.

The income from the logging is returned to local projects, like schools and other community facilities. Individuals earn an income and the whole community gains as well.

Figure 4
The product chain from forest to B&Q store

Rainforest, New Britain, Papua New Guinea
⇓
Selective cutting of trees
(2–3 trees per hectare)
⇓
Timber cut into planks on site
with portable saw mills
⇓
Planks carried to village
⇓
Taken by truck to timber yard
at Bulatawa, 40 km away
⇓
Graded and cut to standard lengths
⇓
Shipped to the UK
⇓
Made into mouldings by FW Mason of Nottingham
⇓
Sold in B&Q stores

> **2** Study Figures 4 and 6 (page 96).
> a) Why do small groups need outside help to get started?
> b) What advantage does their 'certified' timber give them?
> c) Why are more villages in the region wanting to join the project?

Figure 5
Large-scale logging: all the trees are cleared and the forest environment is destroyed

5 Rainforests

unit 10

Figure 6
a) Location map
b) The Bainings Community Forest Project
c) Mobile saw mill
d) Sawn timber being taken away

a) (map)

NEW BRITAIN

PAPUA
NEW GUINEA

AUSTRALIA

BAININGS
FOREST
PROJECT

NEW BRITAIN

PAPUA
NEW GUINEA

N

0   200 km

b)

Logs cut into planks

Increased income:
20 - 30 times as much as
from selling logs

Make use of tree parts
that logging companies
throw away

Long-term future:
sustainable forestry

BAININGS COMMUNITY
FORESTRY PROJECT

News spreads: after 1 year
15 other villages want to
start their own projects

Buyers in other countries
want to stop destruction

Money from timber helps
the whole village –
refurbished church,
new school roof,
new houses

Certificate from independent
organisation to prove the
timber is from a sustainable
forest

c)

d)